Field Guide To

tasmanian
birds

DAVE WATTS

To the late Deny King

Published in Australia in 2002 by
Reed New Holland, an imprint of New Holland Publishers (Australia) Pty Ltd
Sydney • Auckland • London • Cape Town
1/66 Gibbes St Chatswood NSW 2067 Australia
218 Lake Road Northcote Auckland New Zealand
86 Edgware Road London W2 2EA United Kingdom
80 McKenzie Street Cape Town 8001 South Africa

First published by New Holland Publishers (Australia) Pty Ltd
New edition 2002, reprinted 2004, 2006, 2007, 2008, 2010

National Library of Australia Cataloguing-in-Publication Data:

Watts, Dave.
Field guide to Tasmanian birds.

2nd. ed.
Bibliography.
Includes index.
ISBN 9781876334 60 4.

1. Birds - Tasmania. I. Title. II. Title : Tasmanian
birds.

598.09946

Publisher: Louise Egerton
Editor: Howard Gelman
Designer: Roula Doulas
Cover Design: Nanette Backhouse
Reproduction: DNL resources
Printer: Kyodo Nation Printing Services, Thailand

Photographic Credits:

Acknowledgments

During the course of working on this book, I have received a great deal of help from many people and without their assistance this book would not exist.

Firstly, I would like to thank the officers of the Tasmanian Parks and Wildlife Service who have been unfailing in their support of my photographic endeavours: Jamie Bayley-Stark, Peter Brown, Nick Mooney, Mark Holdsworth, Robbie Gaffney, Ingrid Albion and Jenny Burdon. Special thanks to the rangers in the field including Cathie Plowman, Daryl Binns, Brian Carson, Ian Marmion and Jans and Katina Howe.

I am especially grateful to David Baker-Gabb, Kate Fitzherbert, Merrilyn Julian and all the staff at Birds Australia who have been so kind over the years in publishing some of my photos in *Wingspan* and other literature.

Many other people have contributed their time and expertise over the years including Jason Wiersma, Tony and Bev Cawthorn, Scobie Pye, Alan and Trisha Payne, Tim Stredwick and Lynne Davies, Tom Terry, Priscilla Park, Bill Wakefield, Eric Woelher, Tonia Cochran, Menna Jones, Jenny Tulip and Graham and Debbie Roberston. My sincere thanks to them all.

During several lengthy visits to Melaleuca in Tasmania's south-west, I received much help and hospitality from the late Deny King, Janet and Geoff Fenton, Mary and Kylie-Qug King and Peter and Barbara Wilson.

Photoforce in Hobart have handled all my film processing for many years in a most professional manner. A special thank you to Alan, Manu and Brigitte and the rest of the staff who have skilfully converted my film into the birds you see in this book.

Bob Patterson, Sally Bryant, Ray Brereton and Richard Donaghy have received drafts of this book and made many helpful suggestions, for which I am most grateful. Sally Bryant, in particular, helped greatly by providing up-to-date distribution maps and writing the introduction and bibliography.

It has been a great pleasure working with the staff at New Holland Publishers. A special thank you to Gerry Struik, Averill Chase, Howard Gelman and Roula Doulas.

My most sincere thanks go to my partner, Helen Sargeant, who has been my greatest supporter from the very beginning. Without her love and guidance, this book could not have happened.

Foreword

Through its long geographic isolation, Tasmania has become a global centre of bird diversity. There are 12 endemic species of bird that are found in Tasmania, but occur nowhere else in the world. Tasmanians enjoy the year–round presence of nearly 200 other species of Australian birds, but increasing numbers of people from throughout the world travel to Tasmania every year specifically to see the endemic Tasmanian birds.

It is fitting that Tasmania's leading wildlife photographer, Dave Watts, should be the first to bring all of these birds together in one field guide. There are national illustrated field guides to the birds of Australia, but their wealth of detail on the birds of northern and western Australia only serves to confuse the novice Tasmanian bird watcher and encumber the visitor. Regional field guides such as this one are the solution to this dilemma.

I fancy that much of Dave Watt's knowledge of birds has been gained as a by-product of his determination to take the very best photographs of his subjects at various stages of their life cycle. Those birdwatchers who have endured those excruciatingly long hours in hides know what it means to obtain any photographs at all, much less the near-perfect ones that Dave takes. The photographs illustrating this field guide demonstrate the patience and skill of a master of this art.

Nowadays most people no longer have the affinity for the natural world that their ancestors required for their survival, and our senses have been dulled by urban living. However we can rekindle our innate curiosity in nature, and the correct identification of wildlife is a first step to understanding it, and in doing so we can enrich our lives. Out of this appreciation comes a desire to conserve birds and their habitats. Island species are particularly vulnerable to extinction. If we are to ensure that endangered Tasmanian birds such as the Orange-bellied Parrot, Swift Parrot and Forty-spotted Pardalote do not go the way of Tasmania's extinct King Island Emu, then we need to inspire many more Australians to value their natural surrounding. Through his years of dedicated photographic work, culminating in this field guide, Dave Watts has made a significant contribution towards inspiring us to enjoy Tasmania's birds and to strive for their conservation.

David Baker-Gabb
(Past) Director, Birds Australia

Contents

Introduction

by Sally Bryant

Long before European settlement, the indigenous people of Tasmania knew intimately the habits and life history of its birds, both as a resource and as an integral part of their landscape. Depicted in early accounts are the Aboriginal use of Black Swan, duck, shearwater (*yolla*) and all manner of birds that occupied land and sea. Language, ceremony and even the seasonal movement of Aboriginal tribes evolved around the natural elements; people and birds existed together.

The scientific and taxonomic description of Tasmania's bird fauna is interwoven with the early exploration of Australia as the great southern continent. It began with the voyages during the mid-1600s to early 1800s by Dutch, French and British explorers who were charting the coast and sparring for territorial ownership. Adventure Bay, Bruny Island was a favoured anchorage for early ships, often having on board highly skilled naturalists like Baudin, Tobin and La Billardiere who energetically procured large natural history collections for dispatch to Europe. This rich and colourful portrayal symbolises the historical and scientific importance of Tasmania's birds; a heritage which continues today.

Few locations in the world offer over 220 species of resident or regular visitor, including 12 endemic species, all within two to three hours travel of a major centre and nestled among breathtaking wilderness and world heritage scenery. Although Tasmania has a comparatively small land mass, it is an island of some 5400 km of coastline and over 350 offshore islands, including sub-antarctic Macquarie Island. The landscape is dominated by rivers and lakes, and traversed by rugged mountain ranges with spectacular snow-covered peaks. Habitats range from coastal heaths including vast button-grass plains of the south-west, wetlands, estuaries, dry and wet eucalypt forests and ancient rainforests of myrtle, sassafras and huon pine.

Tasmania experiences a humid climate ranging from wet and cold in the west to warm and dry in the east. While the broad distribution of species is reflected by this climate, it is more the expanse of sea and the mosaic of micro-habitats from gully to ridgetop that determines where birds are found. Many of our species are ubiquitous and common, like the Forest Raven, Masked Lapwing and Grey Shrike-thrush—even the Sulphur-crested and Yellow-tailed Black-Cockatoos can be heard across the Tasmanian landscape.

The land bridge between Tasmania and mainland Australia last flooded about 10 000 years ago, leaving the islands of eastern and western Bass Strait as stepping stones and natural barriers to bird movement. These islands are the favoured spots of the Cape Barren Goose, Little Penguin and Golden-headed Cisticola. They also contain huge colonies of the Short-tailed Shearwater (*yolla* or Tasmanian Muttonbird), which provide a magnificent spectacle returning to nest sites after their winter migration to the Bering Sea. Our offshore islands are wild, exciting places. Over half the world's compliment of albatross breed or regularly visit our waters. With the onset of spring over 20 commuters return to the mainland from across Bass Strait, including the Satin Flycatcher, Black-faced Cuckoo-Shrike (summer bird), four species of cuckoo and even the tiny Grey Fantail weighing less than 8 grams.

Our coastal heaths and button-grass plains, with over a million hectares protected in reserve, are a haven for the Southern Emu-wren, Striated Fieldwren, Tawny-crowned Honeyeater and the unusual Ground Parrot, heard calling only at dawn and dusk. Tasmania's waterways and estuaries are rich in bird life, with ten wetland sites recognised as internationally significant (Ramsar sites) and 92 as nationally important. Our sandy beaches and coasts, many pristine and uninhabited, are breeding grounds for the nationally threatened species, the Hooded Plover and Little Tern, and are also rich feeding areas for about 14 species of palaearctic migrants traversing the east Asian–Australasian flyway. The mudflats and tidal bays of Orielton Lagoon (south-east) and Boullanger Bay (north-west) are favourites for Eastern Curlew, Whimbrel, Golden Plover and stint, though there are always newcomers to excite.

Tasmanian forests and woodlands are the stronghold for the Beautiful Firetail, Masked Owl, Southern Boobook and the Grey Goshawk which, in its pure white form, favours the blackwood swamps of the north-west. The endemic subspecies of Wedge-tailed Eagle is nationally threatened through persecution, land clearing and loss of traditional nest sites.

The most important component of Tasmanian bird assemblage is its 12 endemic species. An analysis of global bird patterns shows that species of restricted range tend to occur together in places such as islands or isolated habitats. Boundaries of these natural groupings have been identified as Endemic Bird Areas (EBAs) and in total there are 218 EBAs recognised throughout the world as being the centres for bird diversity. Tasmania in its entirety is recognised as an EBA and is ranked with locations such as Amazonian Brazil, Galapagos and Mauritius. This ranking is further recognition of the importance and significance of our unique bird fauna.

All except two of our 12 endemic species are relatively widespread and easy to find. The Black Currawong with its inquisitive eye and mechanical grating call, described by Gould as 'a hand organ out of tune', is typically a bird of the wet and alpine areas of Tasmania. In contrast, the Yellow Wattlebird, Australia's largest honeyeater, prefers drier low altitude woodland. A further three endemic honeyeaters are all generally widespread in shrubby woodland and forest throughout Tasmania. They can be identified in close proximity, the sedentary Yellow-throated Honeyeater either singularly or in pairs, while the Black-headed and Strong-billed Honeyeaters move in small flocks. Strong-billed Honeyeaters rifle under the bark of eucalypts as they scale the trunks like treecreepers.

The 'cossick' call of the Green Rosella with its cloak of blues, greens and yellow is our own contribution to Australia's colourful rosella assemblage. The Tasmanian Thornbill often overlaps in range with the Brown Thornbill but boasts white flanks and undertail coverts and a sweeter, melodic song. The thornbills are sprightly and active, often preferring dense thickets and low shrub to heavily timbered areas. Filling a similar niche, but usually on the forest floor is the Tasmanian Scrubwren, a bold, busy little bird with a diagnostic white eye stripe and wing spots. The Scrubtit likewise spends most of its time foraging treecreeper-like on tree trunks, but prefers the seclusion of wet ferny gullies where it is particularly cryptic and shy. The Tasmanian Native-hen or 'narkie' can often be seen grazing on roadside verges or in open paddocks. Its extraordinary hacksaw call rising to fever pitch, and intricate social system of 'male harems' make it a fascinating species to study. The stout and robust Dusky Robin prefers lightly timbered woodlands where it can often be seen perching and swooping in typical robin style.

Finally, the endemic Forty-spotted Pardalote, is one of three pardalote species in Tasmania but unlike the others, is totally restricted to patches of dry forest along the east coast, particularly on Maria Island and Bruny Island. Quite different in habit from the Spotted or Striated Pardalote, the Forty-spot is sedentary, shy and unobtrusive, with its soft 'where...where' call and reluctance to move from the white gum canopy.

This Tasmanian photographic guide is an invaluable resource to all those who love and watch birds. Its compact size, portability and easy-to-find sections make it ideal to either study at leisure or to frantically flip the pages to identify what has so quickly passed. Dave Watts' photographs not only represent the very best in natural history photography but portray the magnificence and splendour of Tasmania's birds. His passion and skill, like that of the early naturalists, reflects our priceless heritage. Enjoy all that it offers and all that it represents.

Quail, Ducks, Geese & Grebes

Stubble Quail

Coturnix pectoralis

Family: Quail, Pheasants and Fowls; Phasianidae

Identification: *170–190mm*. The only quail with thick black streaks on the breast and flanks. Male has a rich buff throat and whitish eyebrow. Grey-brown back has overlying pale streaks and bars. Female is larger, has a pale throat with fawn underparts and darker mottling and streaks.

Habits: Occurs singly or in small coveys, generally hidden in thick cover. Flight is swift and straight with rapid wing whirring. Often runs quickly.

Voice: Clear, sharp 'pippy-weet', also deep purring.

Habitat: Coarse grasslands, cereal crops and other pastures.

Breeding: Nest is a scrape in the ground under a grass clump or lined with grass. Eggs: 6–10.

Distribution: Australia (including Tasmania). Now seen rarely in Tasmania but common on King Island.

Where to see: King Island.

Brown Quail
Coturnix ypsilophora

Family: Quail, Pheasants and Fowl; Phasianidae

Identification: *170–210mm*. A large, plump quail with variable plumage. Has barred underparts, but these are not streaked as in the Stubble Quail. Male plumage has rufous and black feathers on the back and wings that are covered with fine silver streaks. Female is paler overall and larger than the male, with heavier dark mottling on the upperparts.

Habits: Occurs singly or in small coveys. Runs in quick spurts with neck outstretched. When flushed, bursts into explosive flight.

Voice: A fairly loud ascending 'f-fweep' or 'tu-wee'.

Habitat: Wet rank grassland or swamps, also stubble and thick pasture.

Breeding: Nest is a scrape in the ground under a grass clump or similar, lined with grass and leaves. Eggs: 7–12.

Distribution: New Guinea, Australia (including Tasmania). Introduced to New Zealand and Fiji. Common in suitable habitat.

Where to see: Flinders and other Furneaux islands, Hazards Lagoon surrounds, Freycinet NP.

California Quail

Callipepla californica

Family: Quail, Pheasants and fowl; Phasianidae

Identification: *230–240mm*. A distinctive, large quail with a long, black teardrop-shaped head-plume. Male has a chestnut crown and a black throat with a white border. Grey-brown above. Grey below, with white streaks on the flanks. Female has a smaller head-plume and duller plumage without the black-and-white face pattern.

Habits: Occurs in small or large groups or coveys.

Voice: A plaintive 'qua-quergo'.

Habitat: Coarse grassland, tea-tree scrub and stubble.

Breeding: Nest is a scrape in the ground lined with grass. Eggs: 10–18.

Distribution: Native of far western USA. Introduced to New Zealand and Tasmania where it remains only on King Island. Other introductions have failed on the Tasmanian mainland.

Where to see: King Island.

Blue-billed Duck

Oxyura australis

Family: Swans, Ducks and Geese; Anatidae

Identification: *350–440mm*. A small, dark diving duck. Male has overall rich chestnut body with a black head and pale blue dished bill. Black tail, which often rests in water or raised in a stiff fan. Female is dark brown with fine buff barring.

Habits: Often solitary or in small groups. Secretive. Dives frequently.

Voice: Male makes a low-pitched rattle, generally during display. The female makes a soft quack.

Habitat: Deep freshwater swamps with dense vegetation.

Breeding: Nest of grass or reed with little down, often with a canopy, in dense vegetation on water or on ground close to water. Eggs: 5–7.

Distribution: Extreme south-west and south–east mainland Australia and Tasmania, where it is rare.

Where to see: Asbestos Range NP, Lake Dulverton when flooded, Rostrevor Lagoon.

Musk Duck

Biziura lobata

Family: Swans, Ducks and Geese; Anatidae

Identification: *470–730mm*. An unusual, large diving duck. Male is large, dark grey-brown duck with a large lobe hanging below its dark triangular bill. Female is smaller with no obvious lobe under the bill. The stiff-pointed tail feathers are dark and often rest in the water.

Habits: Frequently dives when feeding. Displaying male kicks water backwards, fans its tail over its back and expands the bill lobe in a spectacular manner. Often sits low in the water.

Voice: Male makes a loud whistle and grunt following a deep 'plonk'.

Habitat: Deep water swamps with dense vegetation. Lakes and estuaries.

Breeding: Nest is a flimsy cup of plant matter, with canopy, among rushes etc. Eggs: 1–3.

Distribution: South-west and south-east mainland Australia and Tasmania. Common and nomadic.

Where to see: The lagoon in Asbestos Range NP, Orielton Lagoon, Derwent River at Bridgewater.

Black Swan
Cygnus atratus

Family: Swans, Ducks and Geese: Anatidae.

Identification: *1100–1400mm.* An unmistakable large, all-black waterbird with white primary feathers, which are obvious in flight. Bill is red with a white patch towards the tip.

Habits: Seen singly, in small family groups or in large flocks. Nomadic.

Voice: A far-reaching musical trumpet, often heard at night and during flight.

Habitat: Wetlands, lagoons and farm dams. Also pastures and mudflats.

Breeding: Nest is a very large heap of reeds and waterweed on islands or in water. Often in groups or colonies. Eggs: 3–7.

Distribution: Australia, including Tasmania where it is abundant. Introduced to New Zealand.

Where to see: Wetlands, lagoons and farm dams anywhere. Huge numbers occur at Moulting Lagoon on the east coast and Flinders Island lagoons. Asbestos Range NP, Tamar Wetlands, Gould's Lagoon, Derwent River at Bridgewater and Huon River.

Cape Barren Goose

Cereopsis novaehollandiae

Family: Swans, Ducks and Geese; Anatidae

Identification: *750–1000mm*. A distinctive, large pale grey goose with a large yellow cere and a short black bill. Squarish black tail, obvious in flight. Sturdy reddish legs.

Habits: Usually seen grazing in pairs or flocks (in winter) in open pastures.

Voice: Loud deep grunt or honk.

Habitat: Offshore islands with pasture, tussocks and scrub. Also farm pastures with clover and grasses. Farm dams and other wetlands.

Breeding: Nest is a shallow depression lined with grass and down. Eggs: 3–6.

Distribution: Coastal southern Australia (including Tasmania). Strongholds include islands off South Australia and in Bass Strait. Common within range.

Where to see: Maria Island NP, Flinders Island and nearby islands, Cape Portland, Three Hummock Island.

Australasian Shelduck

Tadorna tadornoides

Family: Swans, Ducks and Geese; Anatidae

Identification: *550–730mm.* A brightly coloured, large-bodied duck with a small head and bill. Male has a black head, bill and neck with a white neck-ring and cinnamon-coloured breast. Female is smaller, has a chestnut breast and a conspicuous white eye-ring around the base of the bill.

Habits: Often seen in pairs or small family parties, grazing in the open. Strong flight with slow wing beats. Often flies in long lines or V-formation. Note broad white forewing.

Voice: Males make a low zizzing grunt. Females make a loud 'ong-ownk'.

Habitat: Shallow wetlands, lagoons, farm dams, pasture. Sometimes seen at sea.

Breeding: Nest is usually in tree hollow or under vegetation lined with down. Eggs: 8–12.

Distribution: South-west and south-east mainland Australia and Tasmania. Uncommon.

Where to see: Asbestos Range NP, Moulting Lagoon, Orielton Lagoon, Cape Portland.

Australian Wood Duck

Chenonetta jubata

Family: Swans, Ducks and Geese; Anatidae

Identification: *440–500mm*. Medium-sized duck with a long neck and short, dark bill. Male has a chocolate-brown head and neck with a short dark mane. Body and wings are mainly pale grey. Breast is speckled brown. Undertail and belly are black. Black wing-tips are distinctive in flight. White patch near the rear edge of the secondaries. Female is mottled-brown, white undertail and belly, and lacks a mane; white line above and below the eye.

Habits: Typically seen in pairs or flocks perched on land close to farm dams and lakes. Grazes near water at dawn and dusk.

Voice: A distinctive drawn-out nasal 'gnow' rising at the end.

Habitat: Dams, lakes, wetlands, close to pasture with scattered woodland.

Breeding: Nests in a tree hollow, which is lined with down. Eggs: 8–11.

Distribution: Mainland Australia, mainly in south–east and south-west. Also breeds in Tasmania where it is increasing and becoming common.

Where to see: Farm dams and wetlands anywhere in the east and midlands. Flocks often seen at the lagoon in Asbestos Range NP.

Mallard
Anas platyrhynchos

Family: Swans, Ducks and Geese; Anatidae

Identification: *550–650mm.* The largest and best known of the dabbling ducks. Male has a glossy green head with a yellow bill and white neck-ring. Body is plump with a reddish brown breast. Grey wings. Purple-blue speculum. White tail with black under tail. Orange feet. Female is similar to Black Duck, pale brown overall with darker mottling and dark culmen on the dull orange bill. White underwing in flight.

Habits: Crossbreeds with Black Duck. Rapid flight.

Voice: Male makes a thin, high-pitched whistle and a low 'reeb'. Female makes a descending loud 'quack, quack-quack', often repeated.

Habitat: Almost any freshwater wetland but usually lakes, dams and rivers.

Breeding: Nest of reeds or grass, lined with down, on the ground in dense vegetation. Often near water. Eggs: 6–15.

Distribution: South-west and south-east mainland Australia and Tasmania where it has been introduced. Uncommon.

Where to see: Derwent River near Hobart.

Pacific Black Duck

Anas superciliosa

Family: Swans, Ducks and Geese; Anatidae

Identification: *500–600mm*. Large dabbling duck; the typical wild duck of Australia. Sexes similar. Body dark brown, feather margins paler. Head pattern is unmistakable: a buff face with two dark stripes, crown blackish, bill dark grey. Purple-green speculum.

Habits: Dabbles and 'up-ends' in shallows. Perches on logs in water. Nomadic.

Voice: Male utters soft, three-noted 'quack'. The female makes a loud descending 'quack quack', repeated.

Habitat: Most wetlands, farm dams and swamps.

Breeding: Nest is a grass cup under vegetation or in a tree hollow lined with down. Eggs: 7–10.

Distribution: Mainland Australia and Tasmania. Common to abundant.

Where to see: Throughout Tasmania.

Australian Shoveler

Anas rhynchotis

Family: Swans, Ducks and Geese; Anatidae

Identification: *450–530mm.* Medium-sized duck, which sits low in the water. Large spoon-like bill and a low sloping forehead. Male has a glossy blue-grey head with a white crescent behind the bill and yellow eyes. Forewing and shoulders pale blue-grey. Female has sombre mottled-brown plumage with grey-green feet. Male in eclipse plumage is similar to female except it has orange feet.

Habits: Seen far from shore, in pairs or small groups. Wary. Noisy flight.

Voice: Male makes a soft 'took took'. Female makes a low 'quack quack'.

Habitat: Most wetlands. Prefers large vegetated swamps.

Breeding: Nest of grass lined with down, in thick vegetation or in a tree hollow. Near water. Eggs: 8–10.

Distribution: South-west, south-east and east mainland Australia, also Tasmania. Uncommon.

Where to see: The lagoon in Asbestos Range NP, Moulting Lagoon, the Derwent River at Bridgewater.

Grey Teal

Anas gracilis

Family: Swans, Ducks and Geese; Anatidae

Identification: *360–480mm*. A small, mottled grey-brown duck. Similar to female Chestnut Teal except Grey Teal has a lighter throat and face. Sexes are similar. Narrow white wing-stripe and thin white wedge in armpit is visible in flight.

Habits: A gregarious and nomadic duck seen in small groups often intermixed with the Chestnut Teal.

Voice: Male utters a clear 'pip'. Female makes a wild chuckle.

Habitat: Any wetland from lagoons and estuaries to farm dams.

Breeding: Nests under cover of a fallen tree or in a hollow lined with down. Eggs: 6–9.

Distribution: Widespread throughout Australia (including Tasmania).

Where to see: Many small dams and wetlands, usually freshwater.

Chestnut Teal

Anas castanea

Family: Swans, Ducks and Geese; Anatidae

Identification: *380–470mm*. Male is a small duck with a dark, bottle-green head, rich chestnut body and a white patch on the flank. Black under tail. Female is similar to Grey Teal but darker and lacking the pale throat patch. In flight, the narrow white wing bar is seen in both sexes.

Habits: Occurs in small parties and large flocks, often intermixed with some Grey Teal.

Voice: Male makes a clear 'pip' similar to the male Grey Teal. Female makes a rapid cackle; higher-pitched and shorter than the female Grey Teal.

Habitat: Fresh and brackish swamps, lagoons, farm dams and estuaries.

Breeding: Nest lined with down in a tree hollow, among rushes or in an artificial nestbox. Eggs: 7–10.

Distribution: South-west and south-east mainland Australia and Tasmania. Common or abundant and nomadic.

Where to see: Moulting Lagoon, Asbestos Range NP, Gould's Lagoon, Derwent River at Bridgewater.

Hardhead

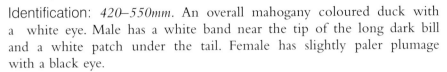

Aythya australis

Family: Swans, Geese and Ducks; Anatidae

Identification: *420–550mm*. An overall mahogany coloured duck with a white eye. Male has a white band near the tip of the long dark bill and a white patch under the tail. Female has slightly paler plumage with a black eye.

Habits: Occurs singly or in groups; large flocks on mainland. Dives frequently.

Voice: Usually silent. A soft 'quack' or a wheezing whistle.

Habitat: Lakes and swamps generally with emergent vegetation.

Breeding: Nest is a neat cup of reeds and stems, often with a roof; under a bush or tree, usually close to water. Eggs: 9–11.

Distribution: New Guinea, Java, Solomon Islands, New Caledonia, mainland Australia and an irregular visitor to Tasmania.

Where to see: Rostrevor Lagoon.

Australasian Grebe
Tachybaptus novaehollandiae

Family: Grebes; Podicipedidae

Identification: *230–270mm.* Small waterbird with a black head and neck. During the breeding season it has a narrow chestnut stripe on the sides of the head and a yellow oval spot between the yellow eye and bill. Grey-brown above with pale chestnut flanks. Tail almost nonexistent and whitish.

Habits: Seen in pairs or small groups on farm dams or lakes. Dives frequently.

Voice: A distinctive chitter.

Habitat: Generally areas of still water, such as farm dams or small lakes, usually with emergent vegetation.

Breeding: Nest is a floating heap of gathered waterweed, which is continually added to. Eggs: 3–6.

Distribution: Indonesia, New Guinea, New Zealand, mainland Australia, and Tasmania where it is rare but increasing, especially in the south-east.

Where to see: Farm dams in south-east especially D'Entrecasteaux Channel area.

Hoary-headed Grebe

Poliocephalus poliocephalus

Family: Grebes; Podicipedidae

Identification: *250–300mm*. Small waterbird. In breeding season, the head is covered with fine white plumes over a grey face. Back is grey-brown, underparts white. Black chin.

Habits: Seen in groups, often up to 100 in winter.

Voice: Usually silent but does have a soft churring call.

Habitat: Farm dams and lakes. Coastal inlets and bays, particularly in winter.

Breeding: Nest similar to Australasian Grebe. Often nests colonially. Eggs: 3–6.

Distribution: Australia, New Zealand (recently established). Common in Tasmania.

Where to see: Farm dams in south-east. Orielton Lagoon, Gould's Lagoon, east coast lagoons.

Great Crested Grebe

Podiceps cristatus

Family: Grebes; Podicipedidae

Identification: *475–600mm*. Breeding adult is unmistakable, with pointed black ear-tufts, used in mutual courtship display. Fine slender bill. White face is framed by a chestnut and black frill, which is much reduced in winter.

Habits: In pairs or small groups, frequent diving. Striking courtship displays.

Voice: A harsh bark or honk. Also a crooning moan.

Habitat: Lakes, reservoirs and bays. Generally prefers deeper water.

Breeding: Nest is a mass of floating waterweed anchored to reeds or other objects. Eggs: 3–5.

Distribution: Europe, Asia, Africa, New Zealand and Australia, including Tasmania where it is rare and nomadic.

Where to see: Lake Dulverton when flooded. Derwent River at Bridgewater, occasionally at Orielton Lagoon.

19

Penguins, Petrels,
Cormorants & Herons

Little Penguin

Eudyptula minor

Family: Penguins; Spheniscidae

Identification: *330–400mm*. The world's smallest penguin. Sexes are similar. Dark blue-grey or blackish above, with silvery-white underparts. Flippers are dark blue-grey with a white trailing edge.

Habits: Swims low in the water. Seen singly or in small groups. Dives and swims underwater superbly. Comes to land and returns to sea during darkness.

Voice: A sharp 'yap'. While displaying and during mating, utters loud braying, wheezing and growling.

Habitat: Seas, coasts and islands.

Breeding: Nest is in a burrow or under rocks or dense vegetation. Sometimes under buildings. Breeds in extensive colonies. Eggs: 2.

Distribution: Resident of southern Australia. Abundant in Bass Strait and around Tasmania.

Where to see: Bicheno area, Marion Bay, the neck on Bruny Island, north coast of Tasmania.

Common Diving-Petrel
Pelecanoides urinatrix

Family: Petrels and Shearwaters; Procellariidae

Identification: *200–250mm.* A small plump petrel. Plumage dark greyish brown above, with white face and underparts. Ear coverts and sides of neck are mottled grey. Legs are set well back; long and blue-grey.

Habits: Occurs singly or in small flocks, often resting on surface of water. Flight is fast and low, with wings in constant motion, flying into waves and under water. Often remaining close to breeding grounds.

Voice: A soft 'koo-koo-aa' in display flight and at breeding colonies.

Habitat: Oceans and islands.

Breeding: Nest is in a burrow among tussocks or rock crevice. Breeds in colonies on islands during winter–spring. Eggs: 1.

Distribution: Breeds on sub-Antarctic islands. Also islands near Wilsons Promontory (Victoria), Kent Group, Councillor Island, Black Pyramid, Georges Rocks, Maatsuyker and Macquarie islands. Fairly common in Bass Strait.

Where to see: Pelagic boat trips, from Eaglehawk Neck and Port Arthur.

Southern Giant-Petrel

Macronectes giganteus

Family: Petrel and Shearwaters; Procellariidae

Identification: *820–980mm*. Size of a small albatross but heavier. Heavy straw-coloured bill with a pale greenish tip. Dark phase has dark brown body with a paler neck and a whitish head. Most birds around Tasmania are juveniles seen mainly during winter. The rare white phase has a few dark spots.

Habits: Usually solitary but gathers in groups for feeding at a carcass. Follows ships, scavenging for scraps.

Habitat: Oceans.

Breeding: Nests in loose colonies on sub-Antarctic islands, including Macquarie Island, and along Antarctic coastlines. Nest is on the ground surrounded by loose vegetation in exposed sites. Eggs: 1.

Distribution: Southern oceans. Common visitor to Tasmanian waters.

Where to see: Pelagic boat trips, such as from Eaglehawk Neck and Port Arthur.

Northern Giant-Petrel

Macronectes halli

Family: Petrels and Shearwaters; Procellariidae

Identification: *900mm*. Very similar to Southern Giant Petrel, except bill is paler and yellowish and tipped reddish-brown or pinkish. Dark head and crown give a capped appearance. No white phase.

Habits: Similar to previous species.

Habitat: Oceans.

Breeding: Nests on sub-Antarctic islands, including Macquarie Island.

Distribution: Southern oceans. Uncommon visitor to Tasmanian waters.

Where to see: Pelagic boat trips, such as from Eaglehawk Neck and Port Arthur.

Cape Petrel

Daption capense

Family: Petrels and Shearwaters; Procellariidae

Identification: *350–420mm*. A plump black-and-white chequered petrel. Unmistakable. Sexes are similar. Head is dark grey-brown. Back and wings are a boldly chequered black-and-white. Tail is white with a dark brown tip.

Habits: A gregarious feeder that follows ships for scraps. Fast, low flight with quick wing beats. Frequently dives.

Habitat: Oceans.

Breeding: Nests in colonies on rock ledges. Eggs: 1.

Distribution: Southern oceans. Breeds around Antarctic coast and on most islands south of 45°S. A common visitor to Tasmanian waters mainly during winter.

Where to see: Pelagic boat trips, such as from Eaglehawk Neck and Port Arthur.

Great-winged Petrel

Pterodroma macroptera

Family: Petrels and Shearwaters; Procellariidae

Identification: *380–420mm.* A long-winged gadfly petrel with a short, stubby bill. Sexes are similar. Body and wings are an overall dark brown with a lighter face.

Habits: Solitary, avoiding ships. Flight is spectacular, with high-wheeling arcs like a large swift.

Habitat: Oceans.

Breeding: Nests in loose colonies on islands Nest is in a burrow or under a rock or vegetation. Eggs: 1.

Distribution: Breeds on sub-Antarctic islands and on some islands in Recherche group and near Albany (Western Australia). Ranges over the Southern Ocean. A common visitor to Tasmanian waters, mainly during winter and spring.

Where to see: Pelagic boat trips, such as from Eaglehawk Neck and Port Arthur.

White-headed Petrel

Pterodroma lessoni

Family: Petrels and Shearwaters; Procellariidae

Identification: *400–450mm.* Sexes are similar. The only large petrel with a white head, white tail and dark grey wings above and below. Note the black eye-patch. Black bill, strongly hooked.

Habits: Flight powerful, with high wheeling arcs on stiff wings. Rarely follows ships.

Habitat: Oceans.

Breeding: Nests in loose colonies in long burrows on sub-Antarctic islands. Breeds on Macquarie Island. Eggs: 1.

Distribution: Sub-Antarctic oceans. An uncommon visitor to mainland Australian and Tasmanian seas, mainly during autumn and winter.

Where to see: Pelagic boat trips, such as from Eaglehawk Neck and Port Arthur.

Antarctic Prion

Pachyptila desolata

Family: Petrels and Shearwaters; Procellariidae

Identification: *250–300mm.* Sexes are similar. Upper parts are blue-grey. Dark eye-stripe with a white eyebrow. Underparts are white. Similar to the Broad-billed Prion except for the bill, which is blue-grey, narrower and does not show the lamellae when closed.

Habits: Often seen in large flocks. Flight is close to the water's surface in order to pluck plankton. Often found beach-washed. Also dives and swims underwater.

Habitat: Oceans and islands.

Breeding: Nests in huge colonies on islands. Nest is a burrow or cavity among rock and scree. Breeds on Macquarie Island. Eggs: 1.

Distribution: Antarctic and sub-Antarctic oceans and islands. A common winter visitor to mainland Australian and Tasmanian seas, mainly during winter.

Where to see: Pelagic boat trips, such as from Eaglehawk Neck and Port Arthur.

Fairy Prion

Pachyptila turtur

Family: Petrels and Shearwaters; Procellariidae

Identification: *240–280mm.* Small blue-grey petrel (the smallest prion). Differs from most other prions by the more extensive, broad black band on the end of the tail and the lack of distinctive dark shading on the head. Also has a finer and less stout bill than the broad-billed prions.

Habits: Often occurs in flocks. Flight is erratic, buoyant and swift. Flits from wave to wave picking food from the surface of the water.

Habitat: Oceans.

Breeding: In colonies. Nest is in a burrow or small rock crevice on offshore islands. Eggs: 1.

Distribution: Breeds on islands off Victoria and Tasmania (mainly in Bass Strait) such as Albatross Island, Black Pyramid, Flat Island and Tasman Island. Also sub-Antarctic and New Zealand islands. Common.

Where to see: Pelagic boat trips, such as from Eaglehawk Neck and Port Arthur.

29

Sooty Shearwater

Puffinus griseus

Family: Petrels and Shearwaters; Procellariidae

Identification: *450–500mm*. A large, all dark-brown shearwater with silvery underwings. Tail is short and rounded. Similar to Short-tailed Shearwater but the Sooty appears slimmer with a heavier bill and whitish underwing.

Habits: Seen at sea in huge flocks. Swimming shearwaters feed on shoals of plankton, squid or small fish. Flight is strong and swift with long graceful glides.

Habitat: Oceans and islands.

Breeding: Nests in huge colonies, on islands, often shared with Short-tailed Shearwaters. Nest of vegetation in a long burrow, usually below tussocks. Breeds on several islands off New South Wales and Tasmania, including Maatsuyker, Tasman, Breaksea and Green. Also Macquarie Island. Eggs: 1.

Distribution: Southern oceans and islands centred on New Zealand, south-east Australia and southern South America. Common.

Where to see: Pelagic boat trips, from Eaglehawk Neck and Port Arthur.

Short-tailed Shearwater

Puffinus tenuirostris

Family: Petrels and Shearwaters; Procellariidae

Identification: *400–430mm.* Overall a dark smoky-brown shearwater with slightly paler underwings. Bill is slender and dark. Tail is short and rounded. The similar Flesh-footed Shearwater (*Puffinus carneipes*) has a pale bill and feet and a more slender appearance. The Sooty Shearwater has a longer bill and most birds have a whitish underwing.

Habits: Often seen in large or huge flocks offshore or massing in large rafts on the ocean surface to feed on squid, krill and small fish.

Voice: A rapid crooning and wailing usually given during courtship or greeting at the breeding grounds.

Habitat: Oceans, islands and headlands.

Breeding: Nest is in a burrow normally under a grass tussock and lined with grass or leaves, usually in vast, densely packed colonies. Eggs: 1.

Distribution: Breeds on islands and headlands of south-east Australia. Very abundant. Tasmanian population numbers approximately 18 million.

Where to see: Ocean beach Strahan, Bass Strait islands, Cape Deslacs (South Arm), the neck on Bruny Island.

Fluttering Shearwater

Puffinus gavia

Family: Petrels and Shearwaters; Procellariidae

Identification: *310–360mm*. A small shearwater, dark brown above with a white underwing and brownish axillaries. Underparts are white with the sides of the breast and neck smudged grey-brown. Conspicuous brown thigh patch. Legs and feet are flesh-coloured with dark brown outer sides.

Habits: Spends much time sitting on the water's surface, diving frequently for food. In flight the feet protrude slightly. Flight is fast and low, with rapid wingbeats interspersed with short glides.

Habitat: Oceans and islands.

Breeding: Breeds in colonies on many New Zealand offshore islands.

Distribution: During winter it disperses to seas off Australia's east and south coasts. Common visitor to Tasmanian waters.

Where to see: Pelagic boat trips, such as from Eaglehawk Neck and Port Arthur.

Wandering Albatross

Diomedea exulans

Family: Albatrosses; Diomedeidae

Identification: *1000–1350mm.* The largest flying bird. Adults have all-white back, head and bases of the upperwings. Undersides and underwings are white. Bill is large, pale-flesh coloured. Immature has overall dark-brown plumage with a distinctive white face. Plumage becomes progressively whiter with age. All ages have some black to the sides of the tail.

Habits: Occurs singly or in small, loose groups. Flight is masterly. Soars effortlessly on stiff wings with long sweeping glides. Follows ships.

Habitat: Oceans and islands.

Breeding: Most adults breed only every second year. Nest is a muddy pile of grass on the ground. Eggs: 1.

Distribution: Circumpolar. Breeds in loose colonies on sub-Antarctic islands including Macquarie Island. Population is still declining. Common visitor to Tasmanian waters.

Where to see: Pelagic boat trips, such as from Eaglehawk Neck and Port Arthur.

Royal Albatross

Diomedea epomophora

Family: Albatrosses; Diomedeidae

Identification: *1000–1200mm*. Large albatross, similar to the Wandering Albatross but the immature Royal Albatross has all white body with dark upperwings and a black terminal tail band. Adults lack any black in the tail. Long bill with diagnostic black cutting edge to the upper mandible. Black eyelids.

Habits: Follows shipping less than the Wandering Albatross, although it is attracted to offal.

Habitat: Oceans and islands.

Breeding: Breeds only in the New Zealand region, including Auckland and Campbell islands. Population declining.

Distribution: Uncommon visitor to Tasmanian waters.

34

Black-browed Albatross

Diomedea melanophris

Family: Albatrosses; Diomedeidae

Identification: *830–930mm*. A robust mollymawk with diagnostic yellow bill. Body and head are white with dark dusky smudge in front of eye. Back, wings and tail are a dark, sooty brown. Underwings have a white central stripe with broad dark margins. Sub-adult has a horn-coloured bill with a dark tip, also grey-brown smudging on nape and back of neck merging into the collar.

Habits: Follows ships and will scavenge from fishing boats. Roams over vast areas of ocean searching for food. Also frequents inshore waters.

Habitat: Oceans and islands.

Breeding: Breeds annually in colonies. Nest is a large muddy cup with added vegetation, feathers etc. Eggs: 1.

Distribution: Circumpolar. Breeds on sub-Antarctic islands including the Falklands, South Georgia, Heard and Macquarie islands. Abundant globally. Common visitor to Tasmanian waters. Vulnerable.

Where to see: Pelagic boat trips, such as from Eaglehawk Neck and Port Arthur.

Shy Albatross

Diomedea cauta

Family: Albatrosses; Diomedeidae

Identification: *1000mm*. Dorsal surface of wings and back are a dark brownish grey. White rump. Under wings are white with thin dark edges. Face is a delicate grey with a white cap to the head. Bill is a pale greenish grey with a yellow tip.

Habits: Flies over oceans with drooping wings, singly or in groups. Often follows ships and fishing boats.

Voice: Hoarse, guttural calls during feeding.

Habitat: Oceans and open seas.

Breeding: Nests in large colonies on remote islands. Nest is a large cup of mud, droppings and vegetation. Eggs: 1.

Distribution: Breeds on Albatross Island in Bass Strait, the Mewstone, Pedra Branca off Tasmania and in the New Zealand region. Common all year round in seas off Tasmania and south-eastern mainland Australia.

Where to see: Bass Strait ferry trips. Pelagic boat trips. Often seen close to shore in rough seas.

Yellow-nosed Albatross
Diomedea chlororhynchos

Family: Albatrosses; Diomedeidae

Identification: *710–810mm*. The smallest albatross, it has a long, slender, black bill with a bright yellow band along the ridge. The slender head and neck is usually white but sometimes has grey-smudged cheeks. Back, upperwings and tail are a dark sooty brown. Underwings are white with clear, black narrow margins.

Habits: Follows ships and readily scavenges from fishing boats.

Habitat: Oceans and islands.

Breeding: Breeds on the more northerly sub-Antarctic islands.

Distribution: Migrates to Australian waters during winter. Common visitor to Tasmanian seas.

Where to see: Pelagic boat trips.

37

Buller's Albatross

Diomedea bulleri

Family: Albatrosses; Diomedeidae

Identification: *760–850mm*. A grey-headed albatross with a white forehead and crown resulting in a capped appearance. Long, dark bill with a yellow band along the ridge and underside. White underwing has a distinctive pattern of a broad black bar on the leading edge and a thin black bar on the trailing edge. The juvenile is similar to the adult except it has a dark brown bill and grey-brown head and neck.

Habits: Follows ships and will scavenge from fishing boats.

Habitat: Oceans and islands.

Breeding: Breeds on islands in the New Zealand region.

Distribution: Disperses across the South Pacific to Peru and Chile; also westwards to south-east Australia. Regular but uncommon visitor to Tasmanian waters. One individual was recently a resident on Albatross Island.

Where to see: Pelagic boat trips, such as from Eaglehawk Neck and Port Arthur.

White-faced Storm-Petrel
Pelagodroma marina

Family: Storm-Petrels; Hydrobatidae

Identification: *180–210mm*. Upperparts are grey-brown with a distinctive head pattern consisting of a white face with a brown dark smudge through the eye. Underparts are white. Underwing is white with a dark trailing edge. In flight, the square black tail and flight feathers contrast with the grey back and shoulders and pale rump.

Habits: Erratic flight during feeding, with long trailing legs. Rests buoyantly on the surface in flocks.

Habitat: Oceans and islands.

Breeding: In colonies. Nests in a narrow burrow in loose soil. Eggs: 1.

Distribution: Breeds on islands in the Atlantic, also many coastal islands of New Zealand, southern mainland Australia and Tasmania, including Georges Rocks (Mt William NP). Common.

Where to see: Pelagic boat trips, such as from Eaglehawk Neck and Port Arthur.

Australasian Gannet

Morus serrator

Family: Gannets; Sulidae.

Identification: *820–920mm*. A distinctive large, white seabird of southern mainland Australian and Tasmanian seas. Body is white with a buff head. Flight feathers and central tail feathers are black. Similar to the Cape Gannet, which has an all-black tail.

Habits: Often seen fishing in small to large flocks. Flight is graceful. Fishing gannets will plunge-dive from a height.

Habitat: Oceans, coastal seas and islands.

Breeding: In large or small densely packed colonies on islands. Nest is a mound of grass, seaweed and mud cemented together by excreta. Eggs: 1.

Distribution: Coastal waters of New Zealand and southern Australia. In Tasmania, it breeds on Black Pyramid, Eddystone Rocks and Pedra Branca. Formerly bred on Cat Island (Flinders Group). Common.

Where to see: D'Entrecasteaux Channel (Bruny Island Ferry); Mercury Passage (Maria Island Ferry); pelagic boat trips, such as from Eaglehawk Neck and Port Arthur.

Little Pied Cormorant

Phalacrocorax melanoleucos

Family: Cormorants; Phalacrocoracidae

Identification: *550–640mm*. A small cormorant with all-black plumage above and white below. White face extends over the eye to the stubby yellow bill. In breeding plumage, it develops a small spiky crest on the forehead.

Habits: Occurs singly or in groups. Roosts in groups. Perches upright with long black tail.

Habitat: Prefers freshwater, rivers, lakes and swamps etc. Also coastal lagoons and estuaries.

Breeding: Breeds in small or large colonies. Nest of sticks, in a tree or bush; sometimes on rocks. Eggs: 3–5.

Distribution: Indonesia, New Guinea, New Zealand, Australia (including Tasmania). Breeds on Three Sisters Island near Penguin, Tasmania. Common.

Black-faced Cormorant

Phalacrocorax fuscescens

Family: Cormorants; Phalacrocoracidae

Identification: *610–700mm*. A large cormorant with all-black plumage above. The distinctive black crown reaches the eye. Bill, chin and facial skin are black. Underparts are white with black flanks.

Habits: Occurs singly or in small and large groups. Roosts on jetties, buoys and islands. Flight is direct and close to the water's surface, with a humpback appearance.

Habitat: Largely marine. Coastal seas, islands and inlets.

Breeding: Breeds in small or large colonies on offshore islands or stacks. Nests on rocks or ledges. Nest of seaweed, sticks, grass etc. Eggs: 2.

Distribution: Limited to coasts of southern Australia (including Tasmania). Common.

Where to see: Maria Island, D'Entrecasteaux Channel, Hippolyte Rocks, Kings Pier Marina–Hobart.

Little Black Cormorant

Phalacrocorax sulcirostris

Family: Cormorants; Phalacrocoracidae

Identification: *580–640mm.* A small, all-black cormorant including a black face. (The Great Cormorant has a white face.)

Habits: Forms large, compact flocks, especially in winter. Feeds on the water's surface in cooperative rafts of hundreds, diving together in a frenzy for fish. Flight is fast and direct, often in lines or V-formation.

Habitat: Coastal seas, estuaries and inlets. Also inland rivers, lagoons etc.

Distribution: Indonesia, New Guinea, New Zealand and Australia. Regular, uncommon visitor to Tasmania in small groups.

Great Cormorant

Phalacrocorax carbo

Family: Cormorants; Phalacrocoracidae

Identification: *800–1000mm.* A large, black cormorant with a whitish chin and face. Breeding plumage is more glossy, with a white thigh patch.

Habits: Swims low on the water's surface. Dives frequently for fish. Occurs singly or in flocks. Perches on piers, dead trees etc.

Habitat: Inland lakes, rivers and farm dams. Also coastal bays.

Breeding: Nest is a bulky mass of sticks, in a tree, usually in colonies over water. Eggs: 3–5.

Distribution: North-east USA, Europe, Africa, Asia, Indonesia, New Guinea, New Zealand, Australia (including Tasmania). Common.

Where to see: Derwent River at Bridgewater, Tamar River.

Australian Pelican
Pelecanus conspicillatus

Family: Pelicans; Pelecanidae

Identification: *1500–1800mm.* A very large and unmistakable black-and-white water-bird with a huge bill. Male is slightly larger than female. Legs are slate-grey.

Habits: Magnificent flier, soaring to great heights. Nomadic. Perches on dead trees, logs etc in water. Becomes tame if fed.

Habitat: Large shallow lagoons, lakes and estuaries. Inland and coastal.

Breeding: Nest is a scrape in the ground lined with seaweed, sticks etc. Often in large colonies on mainland. Small colonies on Bass Strait islands in Tasmania. Prone to disturbance. Eggs: 2–3.

Distribution: New Guinea, Solomon Islands, Australia (including Tasmania). Breeds on small islands off the northern coast of Tasmania. Uncommon.

Where to see: Huon River, Derwent River at Bridgewater, St Helens, Asbestos Range NP, Little Musselroe Bay, Orielton Lagoon, Little Swanport.

White-faced Heron

Egretta novaehollandiae

Family: Herons and Bitterns; Ardeidae

Identification: *650–680mm*. The common heron of Australia. Plumage is pale grey over most of the wings and body. White face and chin, yellow legs. Juvenile only has a pale face, not white.

Habits: Occurs singly or in loose groups. Feeds in shallow water by careful stalking.

Voice: Harsh croaking.

Habitat: Most shallow water including swamps, lagoons and farm dams etc. Inland and coastal. Also paddocks and lawns.

Breeding: Nest is a loose, untidy platform of sticks in a tree, not always near water. Eggs: 3–5.

Distribution: Indonesia, New Guinea, Australia (including Tasmania). Colonised New Zealand since 1941. Common.

Little Egret

Egretta garzetta

Family: Herons and Bitterns; Ardeidae

Identification: *550–650mm.* A small, snow-white egret with a black bill. Legs and feet are black. In breeding plumage, long plumes develop on the head, back and breast. Identified in flight from the Great Egret by its smaller size and faster wing beat.

Habits: Usually solitary. Feeds with a distinctive and dainty dashing in shallow water, with frequent fluttering of wings.

Habitat: Swamps, estuaries, lagoons and farm dams.

Distribution: South Europe, Africa, south Asia and Australia. A rare but regular autumn–winter visitor to Tasmania.

Where to see: Orielton Lagoon, Moulting Lagoon, Blackman's Bay.

Great Egret

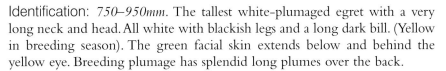

Ardea alba

Family: Herons and Bitterns; Ardeidae

Identification: *750–950mm*. The tallest white-plumaged egret with a very long neck and head. All white with blackish legs and a long dark bill. (Yellow in breeding season). The green facial skin extends below and behind the yellow eye. Breeding plumage has splendid long plumes over the back.

Habits: Usually solitary. Often wades in deep water, freezing motionless at intervals while waiting for prey.

Habitat: Swamps, lagoons, estuaries and farm dams.

Distribution: Almost cosmopolitan. An uncommon but regular autumn–winter visitor to Tasmania.

Where to see: The Huon River, Moulting Lagoon, Blackmans Bay.

Cattle Egret

Ardea ibis

Family: Herons and Bitterns; Ardeidae

Identification: *480–530mm.* The smallest white-plumaged egret. Appears stubbier and has a shorter bill than other egrets. Plumage is all white with a yellow bill. Legs may be dark grey, orange or yellow. In breeding plumage it develops distinctive orange-buff coarse plumes on the crown and nape, breast and lower back. Bill becomes red with a yellow tip.

Habits: Sociable, occurring in small to large flocks, often seen feeding among grazing animals in paddocks.

Habitat: Less aquatic than other egrets. Pastures, paddocks and farm dams.

Distribution: Cosmopolitan, having colonised all continents since 1930. A common and regular visitor to Tasmania, mainly in autumn and winter.

Where to see: D'Entrecasteaux Channel area and north-west coast between Devonport and Smithton.

Nankeen Night Heron

Nycticorax caledonicus

Family: Herons and Bitterns; Ardeidae

Identification: *560–630mm.* A compact, small heron with a large head. Plumage overall is a pale cinnamon to dark brown above, although birds are quite variable, and creamy-white below. Crown and nape are slate-black. Legs and feet are yellow. In breeding plumage, it develops 2–3 long white plumes on the back of the head.

Habits: Mainly nocturnal. Roosts socially in trees or bushes by day. Leaves the roost at dusk to feed.

Habitat: Rivers, estuaries or swamps, usually with forested or vegetated margins.

Breeding: Nest is a platform of sticks often in a bush or tree over water. Colonial nester. Eggs: 2–3.

Distribution: Indonesia, New Guinea and Australia. Rare visitor to Tasmania, although small breeding colonies have occurred on King Island.

Where to see: King Island.

Australasian Bittern

Botaurus poiciloptilus

Family: Herons and Bitterns; Ardeidae

Identification: *650–750mm.* A large, bulky heron with mottled brown plumage, which camouflages the bird well. Bill is brownish. A dark streak extends from below the eye to the side of the neck.

Habits: Solitary or in pairs. Highly secretive, so it is rarely seen except in flight. Heavy, laboured, slow wing-beats. Freezes when disturbed, pointing its bill upwards.

Voice: Male makes a loud, unusual, far-carrying, booming sound during the breeding season.

Habitat: Most wetlands with dense reed beds and rushes. Mainly freshwater.

Breeding: Nest is a platform of flattened reeds and rushes built in dense vegetation over water. Eggs: 4–6.

Distribution: New Zealand, Australia (including Tasmania). Uncommon.

Where to see: Blackman's Lagoon, marshlands on Derwent River above Bridgewater, Moulting Lagoon, Lake Tiberias.

Birds of Prey

Whistling Kite

Haliastur sphenurus

Family: Eagles, Hawks and Kites; Accipitridae

Identification: *500–580mm.* Plumage overall is mid- to dark-brown with pale streaks on the head, neck and breast. In flight, note the longish tail and distinctive underwing pattern of pale body and dark wing tips. Female is larger and heavier than the male.

Habits: Soars effortlessly with slow wing beats, frequently giving a distinctive whistling call. Seen singly or in small groups. Scavenges for carrion and also takes live prey.

Voice: A frequently heard long, shrill whistle, followed by a few short, rapid ascending notes.

Habitat: Open woodland, frequently near lakes, river and other wetlands.

Distribution: New Guinea and Australia. A rare visitor to Tasmania although one or two nests have been built in recent years.

Where to see: Tamar River area.

White-bellied Sea-Eagle

Haliaeetus leucogaster

Family: Eagles, Hawks and Kites; Accipitridae

Identification: *720–880mm.* A large, white eagle with broad, dark wings and a white wedge-shaped tail. Adult is unmistakable. Juvenile is mottled-brown overall with a white tail. Female is larger than the male. Huge talons.

Habits: In flight, frequently soars with upswept wings. Perches for long periods on trees overlooking water. Snatches fish from the water's surface.

Voice: A loud 'ang-ank', two birds often calling together.

Habitat: Coasts and islands, also inland lakes and large rivers.

Breeding: Builds a huge nest of sticks high in a tree, often a Blue Gum in eastern Tasmania or on a cliff on offshore islands. Eggs: 2.

Distribution: India, South-East Asia, Indonesia, New Guinea, Australia (including Tasmania). Common resident.

Where to see: Bruny Island, Freycinet Peninsula, Tasman Peninsula, Bass Strait islands, Tamar River, Arthur River, Strahan and Macquarie Harbour.

Swamp Harrier

Circus approximans

Family: Eagles, Hawks and Kites; Accipitridae

Identification: *500–600mm.* A large, long-winged hawk with overall brown plumage. Breast is pale buff with darker streaks. Note the white rump. Legs are long and yellow with buff trousers. Female is darker and browner. Juvenile has overall rich dark-brown plumage with a pale rump.

Habits: Usually solitary or in pairs, coursing low over paddocks or marshes in search of prey. Flight is buoyant with wings held in a 'V'.

Voice: Usually calls during courtship flight, a short whistling 'kee' or 'keeow'

Habitat: Open country, pastures, crops, reedbeds, coastal wetlands.

Breeding: Nest is a platform of reeds, grasses, etc. on or near the ground in tall grass or in reeds over water. Eggs: 3–5.

Distribution: Europe, Africa, Asia, New Guinea, New Zealand, Australia (including Tasmania). Common. Prone to disturbance during breeding. Most Tasmanian birds migrate north during winter.

Where to see: Common in almost any suitable habitat, mainly spring to autumn. Derwent River above Bridgewater, Moulting Lagoon, Tamar River.

Brown Goshawk

Accipiter fasciatus

Family: Eagles, Hawks and Kites; Accipitridae

Identification: *400–550mm*. A secretive but widespread hawk. Sexes are similar. Adults are grey-brown above with a slate-grey head and chestnut collar. Underparts are cream with fine brown barring. Tail is long and rounded. Obvious supra-orbital ridge over the eye. Female is considerably larger and more powerful than the male. Juvenile (as illustrated) has dark-brown upperparts, heavy streaks on the breast and broad bars on the belly.

Habits: Solitary or in pairs. Largely remains within forest cover, hunting by stealth. Soars in open at times with rounded wings and rounded, fanned tail.

Voice: A shrill chitter 'ki-ki-ki-ki', also a slower 'swee-swee-swee', generally heard near the nest.

Habitat: Forest, woodland, farmland with trees, urban parks.

Breeding: High nest of sticks and twigs, lined with gum leaves. Eggs: 2–3.

Distribution: Eastern Indonesia, New Guinea, Australia (including Tasmania). Common resident.

Where to see: Any wooded country. Often seen in suburbs.

Grey Goshawk

Accipiter novaehollandiae

Family: Eagles, Hawks and Kites; Accipitridae

Identification: *350–550mm*. A thickset and powerful hawk, which occurs in two distinctive colour phases; a grey form and an all-white form. Both colour forms occur on the mainland but only the white form occurs in Tasmania. Bill is black, cere is yellow. Eye varies from yellow to red. May be confused at distance with the Sulphur-crested Cockatoo. Female is much larger than the male.

Habits: Seen singly or in pairs. Typical goshawk flight of soaring on rounded wings, interspersed with fast wingbeats.

Voice: A shrill, high-pitched chatter, also a loud musical 'kuik, kuik, kuik, kuik'.

Habitat: Rainforest, wet sclerophyll forest and woodland. Sometimes seen in more open country.

Breeding: Large nest made of sticks, built high in a tree. Eggs: 2–3.

Distribution: Indonesia, New Guinea, Australia (including Tasmania). Rare.

Where to see: North-west Tasmania.

Collared Sparrowhawk

Accipiter cirrhocephalus

Family: Eagles, Hawks and Kites; Accipitridae

Identification: *290–400mm*. Distinguished from the Brown Goshawk by its smaller size, long tail with squared end, longer middle toe, and the wings appear longer in flight; also its lacks an obvious supra-orbital ridge. Female is considerably larger than the male.

Habits: Secretive. Hunts prey, mostly small birds, by stealth. Waits, perched in cover and flys out and swiftly, snatching prey in mid-air.

Voice: Similar to Brown Goshawk but shriller chatter.

Habitat: Forest, woodland and scrub.

Breeding: Nest of sticks and twigs lined with gum leaves high in a tree. Eggs: 2–4.

Distribution: New Guinea, Australia (including Tasmania). Uncommon resident.

Wedge-tailed Eagle

Aquila audax

Family: Eagles, Hawks and Kites; Accipitridae

Identification: *890–1000mm.* A large, dark raptor with a pale bill and distinctive, long wedge-shaped tail. Adult plumage darkens with age.

Habits: Typically seen resting on dead trees or soaring to great heights with upswept wings. Although a competent hunter, Wedge-tailed Eagles also regularly feed on carrion.

Voice: Normally silent, but a double 'pee-yaa' or a soft yelping 'pseet-you'.

Habitat: Open plains, forests and mountainous country.

Breeding: Nest is huge, made of sticks high in a tree, such as a Blue Gum in Tasmania. Eggs: 1–3. Usually only 1 chick is raised.

Distribution: Australia (including Tasmania). An uncommon resident due to persecution and nest disturbance. Probably only 80 pairs in Tasmania.

Where to see: Mt William NP, Asbestos Range NP, Maria Island and Great Western Tiers, but may be encountered anywhere.

Brown Falcon

Falco berigora

Family: Falcons; Falconidae

Identification: *410–510mm.* A long-legged, medium-sized falcon with highly variable plumage. Sexes are similar. Plumage ranges from dark sooty-brown to reddish-brown above, with underparts ranging from white-breasted to sandy breasted, with or without streaks. All colour phases have a moustachial stripe and dark thighs. The normal form in Tasmania is a brown form.

Habits: Occurs singly, in pairs or small groups. Sits motionless with upright stance for periods on dead trees, fences, power poles etc. Display flights are noisy. In flight, slow wing beats, alternating with glides with wings held in a shallow 'V'.

Voice: A noisy raptor. Coarse cackles and shrieks often in flight.

Habitat: Prefers open country, grassy woodland, paddocks, coastal dunes.

Breeding: Uses disused nest of crows or other raptors, in a tree. Eggs: 2–3.

Distribution: New Guinea, Australia (including Tasmania). Common resident.

Australian Hobby

Falco longipennis

Family: Falcons; Falconidae

Identification: *350mm.* Small falcon with dashing flight. Dark slate-blue above. Crown of head dark slate-grey extending into a moustached cheek stripe. Trousers and underparts are rufous with dark streaks. Eye-ring, cere and legs are all yellow.

Habits: Chases small birds and insects with a swift, dashing flight. Often hunts at dusk.

Voice: Shrill and rapid 'kee kee kee ke kee - - - - -'.

Habitat: Prefers open country with some large trees. Often occurs in towns and cities.

Breeding: Uses a disused nest of a crow or raptor, high in a tree. Eggs: 2–4.

Distribution: Australia, New Britain and Moluccas. Uncommon in Tasmania.

Where to see: Asbestos Range NP, the Tamar River and Midlands area (particularly around Tunbridge).

Peregrine Falcon

Falco peregrinus

Family: Falcons; Falconidae

Identification: *350–500mm*. A well-known large falcon. Upperparts are slate-blue with darker mottles. Underparts are white to creamy-buff with the lower breast and belly having many fine bars. Black crown, cheeks and a moustachial stripe. Female is noticeably larger than the male.

Habits: Occurs singly or in pairs. Flight is magnificent and powerful. Soars with flat wings. Wingbeats fast and shallow. Swoops on prey from height with half-closed wings at high speed.

Voice: A shrill scream or hoarse repetitive 'kek, kek, kek, kek'.

Habitat: Inland cliffs and gorges, coastal cliffs and islands. Also estuaries and wetlands.

Breeding: Nest is a scrape on a cliff ledge. On the mainland, it nests in old tree nests of crows or other raptors. Eggs: 2–3.

Distribution: Almost cosmopolitan, Australia. Common resident.

Where to see: Strezleki Ranges NP, Flinders and Maria islands, Tasman Bridge–Hobart (hunting starlings).

Nankeen Kestrel

Falco cenchroides

Family: Falcons; Falconidae

Identification: *300–350mm.* A well-known, small falcon. Upperparts are pale rufous with black primaries. Underparts are off-white with buff streaks. Male has a grey head, and a grey tail with a black subterminal band. Female has a rufous head and a pale rufous tail with darker bars. Both sexes have a dark moustachial stripe.

Habits: Occurs singly or in pairs. Hovers frequently. Perches on dead trees, overhead cables and power poles.

Voice: A high-pitched repetitive 'kee–kee–kee–kee–kee'.

Habitat: Open country, plains, farmland, coastal dunes.

Breeding: Does not build a nest. Eggs are laid in a tree hollow or in a scrape on cliff ledge, or in the disused nest of a crow or other raptor. Eggs: 3–5.

Distribution: New Guinea, Java, Australia. Rare visitor to Tasmania although more common on King and Flinders Island.

Where to see: King and Flinders Island, Stanley area.

Rails, Waders, Gulls
& Terns

Lewin's Rail

Rallus pectoralis

Family: Rails, Crakes and Hens; Rallidae

Identification: *200–230mm.* A dark-coloured rail with long, slender pink bill with black tip. Upperparts are dark brown with black streaks. Crown and nape are rich chestnut with black flecks. Wings and belly have heavy white barring. Breast is slate-grey with a brown wash. Juvenile is dark grey above and fawn-grey below; it lacks chestnut on the head.

Habits: Very secretive. If flushed, it flies awkwardly with trailing legs. Makes runways beneath marshy vegetation. Crepuscular (active in twilight).

Voice: Loud alarm call 'jick-jick-jic', lasting for several seconds and becoming louder. Also grunting calls.

Habitat: Freshwater and brackish marshlands with dense reeds, rushes or cutting-grass.

Breeding: Nest is a woven cup of rushes and grasses, often with a canopy, in rushes or grass tussock close to water. Eggs: 4–6.

Distribution: New Guinea, east, south-east and south-west Australia (including Tasmania). Uncommon.

Australian Spotted Crake

Porzana fluminea

Family: Rails, Crakes and Hens; Rallidae

Identification: *170–200mm*. This small crake has a short olive-green bill with a red base extending to the upper mandible. Upperparts are olive-brown with dark streaks and spotted white. Throat and breast are dark grey. Belly is barred black and white, undertail white. Legs dull green. Eyes red.

Habits: Occurs singly, in pairs or small groups. Secretive. Feeds in shallow water near cover.

Voice: Wide range of calls including lengthy wheezing, rapid high pitched chatter and sharp 'krr-ek'.

Habitat: Prefers still water swamps, fresh or brackish with dense margins of rushes, reeds, long grass etc.

Breeding: Nest is a woven cup of reeds or grass, lined with grasses, often with an entrance ramp, in rushes or tussock close to water. Eggs: 3–6.

Distribution: South-east, south-west Australia (including Tasmania). Uncommon.

Where to see: Gould's Lagoon.

Spotless Crake

Porzana tabulensis

Family: Rails, Crakes and Hens; Rallidae

Identification: *180–200mm.* A small, dark, crake with no white markings. Upperparts are dark olive-brown. Head and underparts are dark slate-grey. Legs and eye are red. Bill is dark grey. Juvenile has overall paler plumage with almost white throat.

Habits: Very secretive, rarely leaving cover. Occurs singly or in pairs. Constantly flicks its tail.

Voice: Wide range of calls, including a mechanical popping, a single sharp 'kik' and a shrill chatter.

Habitat: Both freshwater and brackish swamps with dense rushes, reeds and other vegetation.

Breeding: Nest is a woven cup of rush grass stems, often on the ground under dense cover, often with frail canopy, near water. Eggs: 4–6.

Distribution: New Guinea, New Caledonia, New Zealand, Fiji, Australia (including Tasmania). Scarce and rarely seen.

Where to see: Gould's Lagoon.

Purple Swamphen

Porphyrio porphyrio

Family: Rails, Crakes and Hens; Rallidae

Identification: *440–500mm.* A large and distinctive water-hen. Head, neck and breast deep azure-blue. Back and wings black. Massive bright red bill and frontal shield. Legs long and pink. White underneath tail coverts.

Habits: Occurs singly or sometimes in large groups. Roosts and climbs in vegetation, rushes or branches over water. When walking, it flicks its tail. When disturbed, it runs or flies with legs trailing.

Voice: Loud, harsh screeching, often at night.

Habitat: Vegetated margins of lakes, swamps and rivers.

Breeding: Nest is a platform of trampled grass stems and rushes and is lined with grasses in reeds or similar. Eggs: 3–6.

Distribution: Southern Europe, Africa, south and South-East Asia, Indonesia, New Guinea, Fiji, New Zealand, Australia (including Tasmania). Common.

Where to see: Derwent River at Bridgewater, Gould's Lagoon, Moulting Lagoon, River Tamar.

Dusky Moorhen

Gallinula tenebrosa

Family: Rails, Crakes and Hens; Rallidae

Identification: *340–400mm.* A familiar dark water-hen. Upperparts are dark olive-brown; dark slate-grey below. Slim red bill and frontal shield, with yellow tip on bill. Distinctive white patches either side of the under-tail. Juvenile is paler overall with a yellow-green bill.

Habits: Occurs singly, in pairs or in loose groups. When swimming, it jerks its head and flicks its tail. Often feeds on land near water. Builds a roosting platform in reeds or bushes.

Voice: Raucous squawks and crowings. Noisy, sharp 'krek'.

Habitat: Freshwater lakes, swamps and farm dams with dense margins of rushes, reeds, shrubs etc.

Breeding: Nest is a bulky platform of aquatic plants in rushes or other vegetation on or near water. Eggs: 6–10.

Distribution: Borneo, Indonesia, New Guinea, Australia. Uncommon in Tasmania, but extending its range. Common on King Island.

Where to see: Farm dams of D'Entrecasteaux Channel, King Island.

Tasmanian Native-hen

Gallinula mortierii

Family: Rails, Crakes and Hens; Rallidae

Identification: *440–470mm.* A large, flightless water-hen. Upperparts are olive-brown and grey, darkening towards the belly. The blackish stumpy tail is usually held erect. Distinctive white patch on flank. Bill is heavy and dull green. Legs are grey.

Habits: Occurs singly or in small family parties. When disturbed, it runs fast, sometimes balancing with short stubby wings, otherwise flightless. Swims readily.

Voice: A wide range of noisy grunts, hoarse rasping and high-pitched alarm calls. Noisy.

Habitat: Grassy paddocks near swamps, lakes and river flats.

Breeding: Nest is a dished platform of trampled rushes, grass or cutting-grass in a tussock or other thick vegetation close to water. Eggs: 4–9.

Distribution: Tasmania only. Common resident.

Where to see: Maria Island, Asbestos Range NP, Cradle Mtn, Lake St Clair and any other suitable habitat.

Eurasian Coot

Fulica atra

Family: Rails, Crakes and Hens; Rallidae

Identification: *320–400mm.* The only water-hen that has completely dark slate, almost black plumage. The bill and frontal shield are white. Legs are blue-grey. Juveniles are grey-brown above, off-white below.

Habits: Seen more often on water than other rails. Often occurs in groups that sometimes form large rafts.

Voice: Wide range of calls including a sharp, loud, 'kyok'. Also loud screeches.

Habitat: Fresh or brackish lakes, swamps, reservoirs and farm dams.

Breeding: Nest is a loose platform of reed stems, sticks or grass, which is built among reeds or other vegetation, sometimes floating on water. Eggs: 4–8.

Distribution: Europe, Asia, New Guinea, Australia (including Tasmania). Common in Tasmania although rare breeder. Nomadic and migratory.

Where to see: Moulting Lagoon, D'Entrecasteaux Channel, Derwent River near Bridgewater.

Painted Button-quail

Turnix varia

Family: Button-quails; Turnicidae

Identification: *165–200mm.* A largish button-quail with an orange-buff shoulder patch. Upperparts have heavy dark-brown mottling and white feather edging. Face, throat and breast are grey with white mottling. Eyes are red. The fine bill is grey. Male is less colourful and smaller than female. White edge to wings visible in flight.

Habits: Occurs singly or in small coveys. Runs when disturbed or will fly some distance to seek cover.

Voice: During display, the female utters a low booming call similar to the Bronzewing.

Habitat: Open shrublands and dry woodlands with extensive ground cover and litter.

Breeding: Nest is a scrape on the ground at the base of tussock, stump etc and is lined with grass and leaves. Eggs: usually 4.

Distribution: East, south-east and south-west Australia (including Tasmania). Uncommon resident.

Latham's Snipe

Gallinago hardwickii

Family: Sandpipers, Curlews, Stints and Snipe; Scolopacidae

Identification: *230–270mm*. A well-camouflaged snipe with a very long straight bill. Eyes are black and set high in the head. Short legs. Crown is dark brown and has a pale split above the bill. Underparts are whitish. Sexes are similar.

Habits: Occurs singly or in small, loose groups. A wary bird, it is usually flushed accidentally, bursting into a fast zigzag flight before dropping back into cover.

Voice: A sharp, rasping 'zhak' when flushed.

Habitat: Freshwater wetlands with dense cover of rushes or grass tussocks, also margins of lakes, rivers and swamps.

Distribution: Breeds in far east Russia, Kuril Islands and Japan. A regular migrant to eastern Australia (including Tasmania) during the southern summer. The population has declined due to habitat destruction and is now stable although generally uncommon.

Bar-tailed Godwit

Limosa lapponica

Family: Sandpipers, Curlews, Stints and Snipes; Scolopacidae

Identification: *380–440mm*. Medium-to-large wader with long, slightly upturned bill, which is pinkish at the base with a darker tip. Plumage is pale grey-brown with darker streaks. Tail is whitish with dark bars.

Habits: Occurs mainly in small flocks. Feeds slowly while probing mud.

Habitat: Essentially estuarine but also found at sandspits and reservoirs.

Distribution: Breeds in the high Arctic. Migrates to the coasts of Southern Europe, Africa, South-East Asia, Australia (including Tasmania) from September to April. Often overwinters. Common summer migrant.

Where to see: Orielton Lagoon, Sorell.

Whimbrel

Numenius phaeopus

Family: Sandpipers, Curlews, Stints and Snipes; Scolopacidae

Identification: *400mm.* Similar to Eastern Curlew, but smaller and with a shorter and less curved bill. Distinctive head pattern of pale stripe through crown bordered by darker stripe and pale stripe over the eye. Note pale rump in flight in some races.

Habits: Occurs mainly singly in Tasmania, sometimes in small groups.

Voice: Distinctive shrill titter 'ti–ti–ti–ti–ti–ti'.

Habitat: Coastal estuaries, mudflats and islands.

Distribution: Breeds far Northern Hemisphere. Migrates to coasts of Americas, Africa, Asia, Australia (including Tasmania). Uncommon summer migrant.

Where to see: Sorell.

Eastern Curlew

Numenius madagascariensis

Family: Sandpipers, Curlews, Stints and Snipe; Scolopacidae

Identification: *550–630mm.* Our largest migrant wader with distinctive, very long down-curved bill, longer and more curved in the female. Plumage overall dark grey to buff with darker streaks and bars. Rump brownish. Lacks the strong head pattern of the Whimbrel.

Habits: Wary. Mainly in small, sometimes large flocks.

Voice: A melodic and haunting 'coorlee'.

Habitat: Coastal estuaries, mudflats and islands.

Distribution: Breeds in north-east Russia and Manchuria. Migrates to coasts of Indonesia, Australia (including Tasmania) during the southern summer. Uncommon.

Where to see: Sorell, Orielton Lagoon.

Common Greenshank

Tringa nebularia

Family: Sandpipers, Curlews, Stints and Snipes; Scolopacidae

Identification: *300–340mm*. A large, lively wader with long, slightly upturned bill, pale at base. Long greenish legs that trail beyond the tail in flight. Overall pale grey-brown plumage with fine streaks and lines. White breast and belly. White rump and lower back are obvious in flight.

Habits: Feeds in shallow water, running and dashing nervously after small fish. Usually seen singly or in small, loose flocks.

Voice: A loud and distinctive 'tew-tew' or 'tew-tew-tew'.

Habitat: Estuaries, mudflats, lakes and swamps. Coastal and inland.

Distribution: Europe, Scandinavia and Siberia. Migrates to Africa, India, South-East Asia, Australia (including Tasmania) during the southern summer. Common.

Where to see: Orielton Lagoon, Sorell, South Arm.

Grey-tailed Tattler

Heteroscelus brevipes

Family: Sandpipers, Curlews, Stints and Snipe: Scolopacidae

Identification: *250–260mm.* A slender, elegant sandpiper shaded a soft uniform grey. Non-breeding adults are plain grey above with white eyebrows almost meeting on forehead. Bill is long, straight and dark grey. Underparts are whitish. Legs are dull yellow or yellow-green. Sexes are similar.

Habits: Occurs singly or with other waders (larger flocks on mainland Australia). Frequently perches on rocks and exhibits nervous head bobbing.

Voice: A drawn-out whistle 'too-eet, too-eet' often in flight. Also a short scratchy 'peep, peepeepee'.

Habitat: Coastal, mudflats and beaches, often rocky.

Distribution: Breeds in the alpine tundra of central eastern Siberia. Migrates during the southern summer to Japan, south-east China, South-East Asia and Australia. Regular but rare visitor to Tasmania, mainly on the north coast.

Ruddy Turnstone
Arenaria interpres

Family: Sandpipers, Curlews, Stints and Snipes; Scolopacidae

Identification: *210–255mm.* A tubby, medium-sized wader with short, dark, wedge-shaped bill. Breeding birds have a bold, black breast and a rufous and black back. Belly and chin are white. Non-breeding birds have grey-brown backs and heads, with paler feather edges with dark centres, but lack the black breast. Short orange legs. In flight, this species shows a striking dark grey-and-white pattern above with blackish rump, conspicuous white wing bar and back, white tail with broad dark sub-terminal band.

Habits: Entirely coastal. Solitary or in small flocks. Feeds by flicking over small stones or seaweed.

Voice: A rapid, clear 'tuka-tuka-tuk-tuk-tuk'.

Habitat: Rocky and stony beaches with seaweed and other debris.

Distribution: Breeds in the high Arctic. Migrates to the coasts of the southern hemisphere during southern summer. Common.

Where to see: Mainly north coast of Tasmania and St Helens Point. Uncommon in south.

Red-necked Stint

Calidris ruficollis

Family: Sandpipers, Curlews, Stints and Snipes; Scolopacidae

Identification: *140–160mm.* A tiny, active, wader with a short black bill, slightly swollen at tip. Black legs. Non-breeding plumage is grey-brown above, with darker streaks and mottling and a greyish smudge on the side of the breast. Dark streak through the eyes. Breeding plumage is a salmon-pink head, neck and breast with chestnut mottling on the back. Narrow white wing-bar shows in flight. Rump and tail have a white margin.

Habits: Occurs in dense, small to large flocks. Feeds mainly with 'stitching' motion, probing into mud. Dense flocks wheel and plunge in flight.

Voice: A constant trilling while feeding; also 'chit' or 'tweek' calls.

Habitat: Estuaries and mudflats.

Distribution: Breeds in northern Siberia. Migrates during the southern summer to the coasts of South-East Asia, Indonesia and Australia (including Tasmania). Very common.

Where to see: Lauderdale, Orielton Lagoon, Sorell, Barilla Bay.

Curlew Sandpiper

Calidris ferruginea

Family: Sandpipers, Curlews, Stints and Snipes; Scolopacidae

Identification: *190–220mm.* A medium-small slender wader with a relatively long, decurved black bill. Non-breeding plumage is grey-brown above, whitish below with a lightly streaked breast. Legs are black and long. White eyebrows are a clear field mark. Breeding plumage is a bright chestnut head, breast and belly. In flight shows a white wingbar and white rump. Juveniles have whitish edges to the back and wing feathers.

Habits: Occurs in small groups or large flocks, often associating with Red-necked Stints. Often wades up to the belly. Wintering flocks often perform active, wheeling manoeuvres.

Voice: A distinctive liquid 'trirup'. Also soft, musical twittering.

Habitat: Estuaries and mudflats.

Distribution: Breeds in the high Arctic of Siberia. Migrates to Africa, India, South-East Asia, Australia (including Tasmania) for the southern summer. Common.

Where to see: Pipeclay Lagoon, Orielton Lagoon, Sorell.

Pied Oystercatcher

Haematopus longirostris

Family: Oystercatchers; Haematopodidae

Identification: *480–510mm*. A large conspicuous wader. Black above with black face and breast. Black band at the end of a white tail. White belly. Legs and stout long straight bill are scarlet. White wing-bar is visible in flight. Sexes are similar.

Habits: Seen singly or in pairs. Congregates in flocks in winter.

Voice: A far-carrying musical piping call, 'keleep'. On breeding grounds, a pleasant 'telee', often repeated.

Habitat: Sandy beaches, estuaries and mudflats.

Breeding: Nest is a shallow scrape on or behind a beach among the dunes. Eggs: 2–3.

Distribution: Common on coasts, particularly in southern Tasmania. Also mainland Australia, New Zealand, New Guinea and Old World. Common resident.

Where to see: Mt William NP, Freycinet NP, Maria Island, Bruny Island, South Arm.

Sooty Oystercatcher
Haematopus fuliginosus

Family: Oystercatchers; Haematopodidae

Identification: *490–510mm.* A large stocky all-black wader with long, stout scarlet bill, eye and eye-ring. Legs are pink.

Habits: Occurs solitary or in pairs; frequently in company with the Pied Oystercatcher.

Voice: A piping call similar to the Pied Oystercatcher.

Habitat: Coastal. Mainly rocky islands, reefs and rocky headlands.

Breeding: The nest is a scrape in the ground among rocks, shingle, pigface or seaweed. Eggs: 2–3.

Distribution: Australia (including Tasmania). Common resident.

Where to see: Bass Strait islands are a stronghold.

Black-winged Stilt

Himantopus himantopus

Family: Stilts and Avocets; Recurvirostridae

Identification: *360–380mm.* An unmistakable black-and-white wader with very long, deep-pink legs. Head and body are white. The black wings are separated from the black nape and back of the neck by a white collar. Long, needle-like black bill. Note the long, trailing legs in flight. Sexes are similar.

Habits: Occurs singly, in pairs or small parties (larger flocks on mainland). Usually seen wading or foraging in shallow water for insects and molluscs.

Voice: A single yelping or yapping note repeated persistently. Higher pitched piping during flight.

Habitat: Freshwater and brackish swamps and lagoons.

Breeding: Nest is a depression in mud, near the waters' edge or on a small island lined with grasses, twigs, leaves and stems of water plants. Sometimes built up in shallow water. Eggs: 4.

Distribution: Almost cosmopolitan. Widespread throughout Australia. A rare vagrant to Tasmania though breeding has occurred recently.

Pacific Golden Plover

Pluvialis fulva

Family: Plovers and Dotterels; Charadriidae

Identification: *230–270mm.* A medium-large, slender plover with a short dark bill. Non-breeding plumage is a grey-brown head, breast, back and wings with pale yellow speckles. Clear white forehead and eyebrow. Whitish belly. Breeding plumage has beautiful black, gold and white speckling on the back and crown, with a black face, breast and belly bordered by broad white streaks on the primaries.

Habits: Occurs mainly in small parties.

Voice: A rapid, musical 'tooweet' or plaintive 'klee-e, klee-e'.

Habitat: Estuaries, mudflats, reefs and islands.

Distribution: Breeds in the high Arctic and western Alaska. Migrates to the coasts of India, South-East Asia, New Guinea and Australasia. Common summer migrant.

Where to see: Cape Portland, Orielton Lagoon.

Red-capped Plover

Charadrius ruficapillus

Family: Plovers and Dotterels; Charadriidae

Identification: *140–160mm.* A small, plump, active wader, also known as Red-capped Dotterel. Upperparts are pale, sandy brown. White elbow. Male has a rufous cap, nape and an incomplete breast band during the breeding season. Both sexes have a broad white forehead. Bill is short and black. Legs are black. Note the narrow white wingbar and dark flight feathers.

Habits: Occurs in pairs or in small groups. Frequently seen running ahead of observer, on beaches. Usually seen with other small waders.

Voice: Range of calls including a rapid trill, shrill alarm call and plaintive 'tik'.

Habitat: Sandy beaches, estuaries, saltmarshes, inland lakes.

Breeding: Nest is a scrape in the sand, often lined with small shells or dead leaves. Eggs: 2–3.

Distribution: Australia (including Tasmania). Common resident.

Where to see: On most beaches, including Scamander and Orford Beach.

Double-banded Plover

Charadrius bicinctus

Family: Plovers and Dotterels; Charadriidae

Identification: *175–190mm*. A small, plump, migratory plover. Non-breeding plumage is dull grey-brown above and off-white below. One or two distinct brown breast bands. Bill is short and black. Legs are dull grey-green. In breeding plumage, adults develop a white forehead and eye-stripe, a black lower throat band and a broad chestnut breast band. In flight, note the narrow white wingbar, dark flight feathers with white bases and that the back is browner than Red-capped Plover.

Habits: Occurs singly or in small groups, often mixing with other small waders.

Voice: A loud high-pitched 'chip-chip'.

Habitat: Estuaries, mudflats, beaches, also inland lakes and grasslands.

Distribution: Breeds in New Zealand. Over-winters in southern Australia (including Tasmania). Common winter visitor to Tasmania.

Black-fronted Dotterel

Elseyornis melanops

Family: Plovers and Dotterels; Charadriidae

Identification: *160–180mm.* A small plover with mottled brown upperparts and a rufous shoulder patch. Face and throat are white, forehead is black and a thick black stripe runs through the eyes beneath a bold white eyebrow. Bill is red with a black tip. Belly is white. Legs are pink. In flight note the white wingbar.

Habits: Nomadic. Occurs singly, in pairs or small groups.

Voice: Single metallic 'pink'.

Habitat: Margins of shallow lakes, farm dams, sometimes tidal saltmarsh.

Breeding: Nest is a scrape in the sand or shingle often lined with small twigs. Eggs: usually 3.

Distribution: Australia (including Tasmania). Recently colonised New Zealand. Common and nomadic.

Where to see: Rostrevor Lagoon, Barilla Bay.

Hooded Plover

Thinornis rubricollis

Family: Dotterels and Plovers; Charadriidae

Identification: *190–210mm.* A stocky plover with a black head, throat and shoulders. Broad white collar at the rear of the neck. Back is pale grey-brown. White underneath. Short, flesh-coloured legs.

Habits: Seen in pairs or family groups running along beaches or flying past observer to settle further along beach.

Voice: Short, distinct piping calls.

Habitat: Ocean beaches and nearby dune systems.

Breeding: Nest is a scrape on the beach often near a log, small plant or sea-weed. Eggs: 2–3.

Distribution: Coasts and islands of south-east and south-west Australia, including Tasmania and Bass Strait islands. Common but threatened by increasing disturbance on beaches by humans, dogs, horses and four-wheel drives.

Where to see: Eastern beaches, Scamander, Maria Island, Mt William NP.

Banded Lapwing

Vanellus tricolor

Family: Plovers and Dotterels; Charadriidae

Identification: *240–270mm.* A large brown-backed plover. Broad black breast band extends to the sides of the neck and under the eyes. Black cap. White line through eye. Bill yellow. Small red wattle at base of bill. In flight, note the broad white wing bar and rump with black flight feathers and black tail band.

Habits: Usually occurs in small parties or larger flocks in winter.

Voice: Plaintive calls often heard at night, 'er-chill-cher' repeated or 'kew-kew, kew-kew'.

Habitat: Plains, open grasslands, paddocks and airfields with short turf.

Breeding: Nest is a scrape in the ground lined with fine grasses. Eggs: 3–4.

Distribution: Southern half of Australia (including Tasmania). Uncommon and nomadic.

Where to see: South Arm, Mt William NP, midlands around Campbelltown, Asbestos Range NP.

Masked Lapwing

Vanellus miles

Family: Plovers and Dotterels; Charadriidae

Identification: *340–380mm*. A large and familiar plover with large, yellow facial wattle. Back brown, white below. Black cap and sides of neck. Spur on forewing. In flight note the white rump, black sub-terminal tail band and black flight feathers. Wings rounded.

Habits: Very noisy, stands erect in groups. Dives at intruders while nesting.

Voice: A loud grating, 'kekekekekek'. Often calls at night.

Habitat: Paddocks, urban parks, lawns, lagoon margins and estuaries.

Breeding: Nest is a scrape in the ground lined with grasses and small twigs. Eggs: 3–4.

Distribution: Two races; the nominate race *miles* occurs in northern Australia. The other race *novaehollandiae* (the Spur-winged Plover), occurs in south-east Australia (including Tasmania). Abundant resident.

Arctic Jaegar

Stercorarius parasiticus

Family: Skuas; Stercorariidae

Identification: *450mm.* A small skua with a small head. It occurs in two colour forms. The non-breeding dark form has overall dark brown plumage with a black head and grey neck, and conspicuous white shafts to the primaries. During breeding plumage it develops a yellow neck collar and two long, pointed central tail feathers, often missing after breeding. The light form has a pale buff throat and undersides.

Habits: Piratic, harrying other seabirds and gulls for food. Occurs singly or in small parties. Follows ships.

Habitat: Oceans and seas. Sometimes enters bays and harbours.

Distribution: Breeds north of the Arctic Circle and northern Europe. Overwinters in Southern Hemisphere seas. Common migrant.

Where to see: Pelagic boat trips.

Pacific Gull
Larus pacificus

Family: Gull and Terns; Laridae

Identification: *580–650mm*. A large gull. Massive, heavy bill is yellow with a red tip. Head and body are white with black back and wings. Legs are yellow. In flight, note the white tail with black sub-terminal band. Juveniles are uniformly mottled brown.

Habits: Occurs singly, in pairs or larger groups. Follows fishing boats. Squid, crabs, molluscs etc. are dropped onto rocks from a height causing 'middens' to develop.

Voice: A loud distinctive honking 'auk, auk' or 'ow, ow'.

Habitat: Coastal. Beaches and offshore islands. Rubbish tips close to the coast in Tasmania.

Breeding: Breeds singly or in loose colonies on offshore islands. Nest is a cup of twigs, roots and grasses on the ground. Eggs: 2–3.

Distribution: Southern Australia (including Tasmania), particularly Bass Strait. Common resident.

Kelp Gull

Larus dominicanus

Family: Gulls and Terns; Laridae

Identification: *550–580mm*. Similar to the Pacific Gull but a more slender bird with a slimmer bill. Main identification marks are the slimmer pale yellow bill with red spot on lower mandible and white tips to the secondaries and primaries showing as white 'windows' at the wing tips when the bird is at rest. Legs are greenish-yellow. In flight, note the all-white tail.

Habits: Occurs in pairs and often flocks during winter.

Voice: A sobbing yelp unlike other Tasmanian gulls.

Habitat: Coastal. Islands, beaches, paddocks and refuse tips.

Breeding: Nest and eggs similar to the Pacific Gull but smaller eggs.

Distribution: South America, South Africa, New Zealand and, from 1930s, southern Australia (including Tasmania). Increasing. Common resident in south-east and east Tasmania.

Silver Gull

Larus novaehollandiae

Family: Gulls and Terns; Laridae

Identification: *380–420mm.* The common gull of Tasmania's coast. Body is white with silvery blue-grey back and wings. Wing tips black with white windows. Legs, bill and eye-ring are scarlet.

Habits: Occurs often in flocks, particularly at refuse tips, fishing ports and freshly ploughed fields.

Voice: A vocal, harsh 'keow' or 'karr', often repeated.

Habitat: Coastal and inland waters.

Breeding: Usually in colonies, sometimes large. On islands, rocks or small peninsulas. Nest is a scrape in the ground lined with rootlets and seaweed among low vegetation. Eggs: 1–3.

Distribution: New Zealand, New Caledonia, Australia (including Tasmania). Abundant and partially nomadic.

Caspian Tern

Sterna caspia

Family: Gulls and Terns; Laridae

Identification: *500–550mm.* The world's largest tern. Unmistakable, during the breeding season it has a massive scarlet bill, a black crown and legs. During non-breeding season the crown becomes streaked with dark brown and the forehead white. Body is white with pale grey back and wings. In flight, note the slightly forked tail with darker wing tips.

Habits: Occurs singly or in pairs. Patrols over water bodies plunging to catch fish.

Voice: A harsh 'kraa' particularly heard near the nest.

Habitat: Coastal and large inland waters, lakes and rivers.

Breeding: Usually singly or in small groups on islands (frequently in a high area). Nest is a scrape in the ground in sand or shingle, or among short vegetation. Eggs: 1–2.

Distribution: Worldwide. Common and nomadic.

Where to see: Almost any coastal area or large inland waters of Tasmania.

Crested Tern

Sterna bergii

Family: Gulls and Terns; Laridae

Identification: *430–480mm.* Commonest Tasmanian tern. Crown black with slight crest at rear, which can be raised. Forehead white. Bill yellow. Body white with pale grey back and wings. Tail forked. During non-breeding, cap becomes mottled with a larger area of white on the forehead.

Habits: Occurs singly or in flocks. Often perches or roosts with gulls on beaches, sandspits or jetties. Graceful flight, often patrols shallow water to feed by plunge-diving.

Voice: A vocal 'kirrick' usually heard near breeding colonies.

Habitat: Coastal, estuaries, tidal rivers and islands. Sometimes inland on large waters or rivers.

Breeding: Often nests in large colonies on islands. Nest is a scrape in the ground or among rocks or low vegetation. Eggs: 1.

Distribution: South Africa, south and east Asia, Australia (including Tasmania). Common and nomadic.

Where to see: Any coastal area.

White-fronted Tern

Sterna striata

Family: Gulls and Terns; Laridae

Identification: *380–410mm*. The largest 'commic' tern. Breeding plumage is a black cap and bill with white forehead. In non-breeding birds the white forehead enlarges. Slightly smaller than Crested Tern. Deeply forked tail. Legs are dark red.

Habits: Occurs singly or in flocks, often with Crested Terns, but more buoyant flight.

Voice: Calls frequently in flight—a rasping, high-pitched 'keek-eet' or 'kee-eck-keek-eek'.

Habitat: Oceanic. Breeds on islands.

Breeding: Nests in small scattered colonies on little islands. Nest is a scrape in sand or shingle. Eggs: 1–2.

Distribution: Breeds in New Zealand. A few pairs breed on exposed reefs near Flinders Island, Bass Strait. An uncommon winter visitor.

Little Tern

Sterna albifrons

Family: Gulls and Terns; Laridae

Identification: *200–250mm.* Small, slim, pale grey tern with white forehead and underparts. Black crown extends in a narrow wedge from the eye to the bill. Bill is yellow, usually with a black tip. Legs are a more orange-yellow. Darker upperparts, black wing tips and leading wing edge separate this species from Fairy Tern.

Habits: Rapid flight with fast wingbeats. When fishing, it hovers with stiff, upheld wings. Seen in small groups or singly, often with other terns.

Voice: Sharp, high-pitched 'kweek'. Excited 'peet-peet-peet' while hovering.

Habitat: Coasts, inlets and coastal lagoons.

Breeding: Singly or in small, loose colonies on beaches, sandspits or islands, often with Fairy Terns. Nest is a scrape in sand or shells. Eggs: 1–2.

Distribution: Rare and endangered in Tasmania, with less than 10 pairs breeding annually. Threatened by increasing disturbance of beaches by humans, dogs, horses and four-wheel drives. Occurs almost worldwide.

Where to see: East coast inlets and lagoons.

Fairy Tern

Sterna nereis

Family: Gulls and Terns; Laridae

Identification: *220–260mm.* Similar to the Little Tern but with a slightly larger, more rounded head and shorter, thicker, orange legs. During breeding it has an all-orange bill and a larger area of white forehead. Cap is black; the black stripe from the black crown to the eye does not extend to the base of the bill. The body is white with soft blue-grey back and wings.

Habits: Occurs singly or in small flocks.

Voice: A vocal 'chi-wik' and excited twittering 'kiri-kiki' repeated.

Habitat: Coastal lagoons, estuaries, inlets and sand spits.

Breeding: Nests in small colonies on sandy beaches or sandspits. Nest is a scrape in the sand. Eggs: 1–2.

Distribution: New Zealand, New Caledonia, Australia (including Tasmania). Threatened by increasing disturbance of beaches by humans, dogs, horses and four-wheel drives. Uncommon and nomadic.

Where to see: North and east coast beaches, inlets and lagoons, also some Bass Strait islands.

Pigeons, Parrots, Owls
& Kingfishers

Spotted Turtle-Dove

Streptopelia chinensis

Family: Pigeons and Doves; Columbidae

Identification: *315–316mm.* A large grey-brown dove with pinkish-fawn underparts. Back of neck is black with white spots. Back, wings and long tail are brown and white.

Habits: Occurs singly, in pairs or parties. Upon alighting, the tail is raised and lowered,

Voice: A mellow 'coo' or 'coocoo'.

Habitat: Parks, gardens and rural areas.

Breeding: The nest is a sparse platform of twigs built in a dense tree or shrub. Eggs: 2.

Distribution: India, Sri Lanka, South-East Asia, south China. Introduced to south-east and east Australia (including Tasmania). Common resident in some areas.

Where to see: Mainly around Hobart and Launceston.

Common Bronzewing

Phaps chalcoptera

Family: Pigeons and Doves; Columbidae

Identification: *290–350mm.* A large, tubby pigeon. Male has a cream forehead with a chocolate-brown rear crown and nape. The eye is dark with a white line beneath it. Upperparts are brown with pale edges to feathers giving a scaly appearance. The breast is greyish pink. Wings have a metallic sheen. Female has a grey forehead, no brown cap and is duller overall.

Habits: Occurs singly, in pairs or small, loose groups. Feeds on the ground. A wary bird that bursts into the air with clattering wings when disturbed.

Voice: A repetitive, monotonous 'oom-oom'.

Habitat: Forest, woodland and scrub.

Breeding: The nest is a sparse platform of twigs and rootlets in a shrub or tree. Eggs: 2.

Distribution: Australia (including Tasmania), also Bass Strait islands. Generally a common resident.

Brush Bronzewing

Phaps elegans

Family: Pigeons and Doves; Columbidae

Identification: *270–320mm.* A plump pigeon, the chestnut-brown on the throat patch, shoulders and back of the neck extends as a stripe through the eye. Male has a yellow-buff forehead with a grey crown. The upperparts are olive-brown with metallic bronze bands on the wing. Female is grey-brown above with no chestnut.

Habits: Occurs singly or in pairs. Feeds on the ground.

Voice: A muffled repetitive 'oom-oom' with a higher pitch than the previous species.

Habitat: Forests, woodland and scrub generally with a dense understorey.

Breeding: Nest is a flimsy platform of twigs and rootlets in a shrub often near the ground. Eggs: 2.

Distribution: South-west and south-east mainland Australia (including Tasmania), also Bass Strait islands. Generally a common resident.

Yellow-tailed Black-Cockatoo

Calyptorhynchus funereus

Family: Cockatoos; Cacatuidae

Identification: *580–680mm.* A large, black Cockatoo with yellow panels in the tail and yellow ear patches. Body feathers have pale yellow edges. Bill is grey. Male has a pink eye-ring and a smaller yellow cheek patch than the female, which has a grey eye-ring.

Habits: Occurs in pairs, and in small and large flocks. Feeds by stripping bark from eucalypts and wattles. Also attacks pine cones and banksia seed. The long tail is distinctive in flight.

Voice: A wailing, plaintive 'wee-yoo' or 'wee lah', also screeching.

Habitat: Forest, woodland and coastal heathland.

Breeding: The nest is in a tree hollow, often high. Eggs: 1.

Distribution: South-east Australia, Tasmania and the larger Bass Strait islands. Common and nomadic.

Where to see: Tasman Peninsula, Freycinet Peninsula, Moulting Lagoon surrounds, Mt William NP and Asbestos Range NP.

Galah

Cacatua roseicapilla

Family: Cockatoos; Cacatuidae

Identification: *350–370mm.* A distinctive, familiar pink and grey cockatoo that has a white crown with a low crest. Male has a dark brown eye. Female has a red eye.

Habits: Occurs singly or in pairs but frequently in noisy flocks. Often feeds on the ground.

Voice: A loud screech or high pitched 'chee-chee'.

Habitat: Woodland, farmland and gardens.

Breeding: Nest is in a hollow tree with bark usually stripped from around the entrance. Eggs: 3–4.

Distribution: Australia. Vagrant to Bass Strait islands. Probably introduced to Tasmania where it is common in some areas near Hobart, Bicheno and Launceston. Increasing resident.

Long-billed Corella
Cacatua tenuirostris

Family: Cockatoos; Cacatuidae

Identification: *350–400mm*. A large, white cockatoo with pink feathers on the throat and short crest. Has a distinctive long upper mandible that can be seen at close range.

Habits: Occurs in small parties in Tasmania or huge flocks on the mainland. Feeds on the ground, usually in the company of Sulphur-crested Cockatoos.

Voice: Loud screeching and quavering 'kurrup'.

Habitat: Open woodland and agricultural land. Crops and stubble.

Breeding: Nests in a tree hollow, usually high. Eggs: 2–3.

Distribution: South-east mainland of Australia. Generally considered to be introduced to Tasmania from aviary escapees.

Where to see: Tasmanian midlands and the Hamilton–Ouse area.

Little Corella

Cacatua sanguinea

Family: Cockatoos; Cacatuidae

Identification: *360–380mm.* A small white cockatoo with a short crest. Bill is small and whitish. Bare, pale blue eye-patch with a pink patch in front of the eye. While it lacks the pink throat feathers of the Long-billed Corella, these feathers are pink at the base. In flight, note the sulphur-yellow under-wings and undertail.

Habits: Occurs in pairs or large, often huge, flocks on the mainland. Flight is direct and fast.

Voice: Very vocal, loud screeching and high-pitched 'wuk-wuk-wuk'. Similar to the Long-billed Corella.

Habitat: Open woodland and agricultural land.

Breeding: Nests in a tree hollow. Eggs: 2–4.

Distribution: New Guinea, Australia (including Tasmania). Generally considered to be introduced to Tasmania from aviary escapees.

Where to see: Midlands and Hamilton–Ouse area.

Sulphur-crested Cockatoo

Cacatua galerita

Family: Cockatoos; Cacatuidae

Identification: *450–500mm.* A familiar all-white cockatoo with a long yellow crest. Bill is steely black. Yellow underwings show in flight. Male has a black eye; female a ruby-red eye.

Habits: Occurs singly, in pairs or large flocks. Frequently seen feeding on the ground. The crest is often raised when alighting and also near the nest.

Voice: A vocal, raucous screech and squawk.

Breeding: Nests in a tree hollow, usually high. Eggs: 2–3.

Distribution: New Guinea, New Zealand, and Australia (including Tasmania) where it is a common resident.

Where to see: Midlands and Hamilton–Ouse area.

Musk Lorikeet

Glossopsitta concinna

Family: Lorkeets; Loriidae

Identification: *200–230mm.* A small lorikeet with a scarlet forehead and cheek patch. Crown is bluish. Overall plumage is green. Bill is black with a red tip.

Habits: Occurs in pairs or small flocks, flying swiftly to feed on blossom, orchards or gardens.

Voice: A high-pitched screech and chatter while feeding.

Habitat: Dry forests, woodlands, roadside plantings and gardens.

Breeding: Nests in a eucalypt tree hollow. Eggs: 2.

Distribution: South-east Australia, including Tasmania, where it is restricted to the drier areas of the east and south-east. Common in some areas. Breeding resident.

Where to see: Hobart airport and South Arm–Rhebon.

Green Rosella

Platycercus caledonicus

Family: Broadtailed Parrots; Platycercidae

Identification: *330–370mm*. A dark rosella that is endemic to Tasmania. Upperparts are dark mottled green. Head is bright yellow with blue cheek patch and red forehead band. Shoulder and leading edge of the wing is blue. Underparts are yellow. Female is duller than the male.

Habits: Occurs in pairs, small parties or larger flocks in autumn and winter. Often seen flying fast and high.

Voice: A loud metallic 'cussick, cussick', often heard during flight. Also a softer, bell-like note is often heard while perched.

Breeding: Nests in a tree-hollow. Eggs: 4–8.

Distribution: Endemic to Tasmania and Bass Strait islands. Common resident.

Eastern Rosella

Platycercus eximius

Family: Broadtailed Parrots; Platycercidae

Identification: *290–330mm.* A distinctive, brightly coloured parrot. Head and upper breast are scarlet with white cheek patches. Upperparts are black with yellow feather edges giving a mottled appearance.

Habits: Occurs in pairs, small parties or flocks during autumn and winter. Frequently seen perched on roadside fences. Feeds primarily on the ground.

Voice: A high-pitched 'pink-pink' heard during flight. Also a mellow 'pee-p-pee' and soft chatterings.

Habitat: Open forest, woodland, parks, gardens and agricultural land.

Breeding: Nests in a tree hollow or decayed stump. Eggs: 4–7.

Distribution: South-east Australian mainland and north and east Tasmania. Common resident.

Where to see: The Domain, Hobart, Seven-Mile Beach, Hobart Airport.

Swift Parrot

Lathamus discolor

Family: Broadtailed Parrots; Platycercidae

Identification: *230–250mm*. A slender parrot with a long, thin dusky-red tail. Overall plumage is bright green, darker above, with a red forehead, throat and a round bill. Also has red under the tail and on the secondaries. The common and greater wing coverts are blue.

Habits: Occurs singly or in small parties; often seen flying at great speed to feed, with much chattering, on eucalypt blossom.

Voice: A distinctive, high-pitched piping 'pee-pit', pee-pit, pee-pit'.

Habitat: Forests, woodlands, parks, gardens and street plantings with blossoming eucalypts. Particularly favours the Blue Gum.

Breeding: Nests in a tree hollow, usually high in a eucalypt. Eggs: 3–5.

Distribution: Summer visitor to eastern Tasmania for breeding. A small population breeds on the north-west coast between Launceston and Smithton. Migrates in winter to the south-east mainland. Common in some areas.

Where to see: Bruny Island, Maria Island, Forest Glen Tea Gardens near Spreyton, Hobart.

Blue-winged Parrot

Neophema chrysostoma

Family: Broadtailed Parrots; Platycercidae

Identification: *210–230mm.* A smallish, largely terrestrial grass parrot with a long tail. Male is olive-green above with a blue and yellow facial band. Broad patch of deep blue on the leading edge of the wings. Lower breast and belly are bright yellow.

Habits: Occurs in pairs, small parties or flocks, often feeding on the ground among grasses, fluttering ahead and perching when flushed.

Voice: A high-pitched 'zit, zit' and double tinkling call in flight.

Habitat: Grassy woodland, heathland and grassy paddocks.

Breeding: Nests in a tree hollow. Eggs: 4–6.

Distribution: South-east Australia (including Tasmania). Common in some areas. Summer migrant.

Orange-bellied Parrot

Neophema chrysogaster

Family: Rosellas, Grass Parrots and allies; Platycercidae

Identification: *200–215mm.* Male is brilliant emerald green above with yellow breast and orange patch on belly. Leading edge of wing deep blue. Frontal forehead band bright blue. Female has duller colouration.

Habits: Feeds on ground in small parties or flocks of up to 40 individuals. Migrates in winter to coasts of south-east mainland Australia.

Voice: Flight call is a metallic tinkling. Alarm call, a rapid buzzing 'zizizizi'.

Habitat: Coastal button-grass plains with patches of forest in south-west Tasmania. Wintering habitat on mainland comprises mainly coastal areas of inlets and lagoons with saltmarsh and low shrubs.

Breeding: Breeds only in south-west Tasmania. Nest is in a tree hollow, normally high. Eggs: 4–6.

Distribution: Rare and endangered, possibly only 200 individuals in the wild. Recent increase. Winters on coasts of Victoria and South Australia.

Where to see: Melaleuca, South-West World Heritage Area, where a public hide overlooks a feeding station for Orange-bellied Parrots.

Ground Parrot

Pezoporus wallicus

Family: Broadtailed Parrots; Platycercidae

Identification: *290–320mm.* A medium-sized, bright green parrot with a long tail. Upperparts are yellow-green with dark barring. The long tail is green with faint yellow barring. Small red forehead patch.

Habits: Occurs singly, in pairs or small, loose parties. Secretive and somewhat nocturnal, it spends much time hidden in low vegetation.

Voice: Mostly heard at dawn or dusk. Four to seven high-pitched, sweet, ascending bell-like notes: 'tee, tee, tee, tee, tee'.

Habitat: Densely vegetated coastal heaths, swamps and button-grass plains.

Breeding: Nest is a shallow depression lined with chewed grass stems, hidden under a grass tussock or low bush. Eggs: 3–4.

Distribution: Coastal south-west and south-east Australia and western Tasmania. Also Hunter Island in Bass Strait. Scarce resident. South-west Tasmania is a stronghold.

Where to see: Button-grass plains and low heathland near Strathgordon, Port Davey, Cockle Creek and Strahan airfield.

Pallid Cuckoo

Cuculus pallidus

Family: Cuckoos; Cuculidae

Identification: *290–330mm.* A slender, medium-to-large cuckoo with a white spot on the nape. Adult is grey-brown above and underparts are pale grey. Eye-ring is yellow with dark grey eye-stripe. The long tail is dark grey with white notches. Immature and sub-adult is mottled brown above with brown streaks on the head.

Habits: Occurs singly or in pairs. The fast flight is slightly undulating and falcon-like. Note the pointed wings and, upon alighting on a perch, the tail is frequently raised and lowered.

Voice: Males make a familiar and persistent series of rising notes. Also a wild, excited 'crookya, crookya' is uttered while chasing a female.

Habitat: Open woodland, gardens and agricultural land with trees.

Breeding: No nest built but eggs are laid singly in nests of other species, mainly cup nests of honeyeaters but also cuckoo-shrikes, orioles, Magpie Larks, woodswallows and flycatchers.

Distribution: Australia (including Tasmania). A regular spring and summer migrant. Relatively common.

Fan-tailed Cuckoo

Cacomantis flabelliformis

Family: Cuckoos; Cuculidae

Identification: *250–280mm.* A slender blue-grey cuckoo with a warm buff to dull rufous breast. The long, wedge-shaped tail has distinctive white notches down the sides. Eye is black with a yellow eye-ring. Juvenile is brown above with finely barred underparts. Note the pale wingbar in flight.

Habits: Occurs singly or in pairs. Often sits on a low, prominent perch. Flight is gently undulating.

Voice: Calls, day and night, a far-carrying, plaintive descending trill 'peeeeeeeeer'.

Habitat: Forest and woodland; also more open wooded country, parks and gardens.

Breeding: No nest is built. Eggs are laid singly, mainly in domed nests of scrubwrens, thornbills or fairy-wrens.

Distribution: New Guinea, Solomon Islands, New Caledonia, eastern and southern mainland Australia. A summer visitor to Tasmania.

Horsfield's Bronze-Cuckoo

Chrysococcyx basalis

Family: Cuckoos; Cuculidae

Identification: *150–170mm*. A small, dull-bronze cuckoo with bright rufous bases to the outer tail feathers. Breast has bold, incomplete bars on each side. Eyes are dark with pale eyebrows curving down the neck.

Habits: Occurs singly or in pairs. Sometimes seen perched quietly on transmission wires or fences.

Voice: A long, descending and frequently repeated 'tseeeeeyou'.

Habitat: Open woodland, scrub, parks and gardens.

Breeding: No nest is built. Eggs are laid singly, mainly in domed nests of thornbills, fairy-wrens, also open cup-nests of honeyeaters and flycatchers.

Distribution: New Guinea, Indonesia, Australia. A summer visitor to Tasmania. Uncommon.

Shining Bronze-Cuckoo

Chrysococcyx lucidus

Family: Cuckoos; Cuculidae

Identification: *160–180mm*. The Australian race is *plagosus*. A metallic green-bronze cuckoo with complete coppery-bronze bars on white underparts. Cap and nape is copper. New Zealand race *lucidus* has prominent white flecks on the forehead and the bars are iridescent green.

Habits: Occurs singly or in pairs. Generally inconspicuous except during the breeding season, when males call from an elevated perch.

Voice: A distinct, high-pitched whistle 'peee, peee, peee', each note rising at end.

Habitat: Forest, woodland, parks, gardens and scrub. Occupies less open country than Horsfield's Bronze Cuckoo.

Breeding: No nest is built. Eggs are generally laid in the domed nests of thornbills, fairy wrens and scrubwrens.

Distribution: New Guinea, Australia (including Tasmania). Locally common.

Southern Boobook

Ninox novaeseelandiae

Family: Hawk-owls; Strigidae

Identification: *300–350mm*. A familiar, small, brown hawk-owl with pale green-yellow eyes surrounded by dark patches with pale borders. In Tasmania the eyes are more yellow. Large white spots on wing scapulars. Breast and belly whitish with variable brown streaks. Legs fully feathered. Tasmanian birds are generally darker than those on the mainland.

Habits: Occurs singly or in pairs. Usually feeds at dusk from a prominent perch.

Voice: A familiar, high-pitched 'boo-book' or 'mo-poke', which is repeated at intervals.

Habitat: Forest, woodland, parks, gardens and scrub.

Breeding: Nests in a tree hollow. Eggs: 2–3.

Distribution: New Guinea, New Zealand and Australia, incuding Tasmania and the Bass Strait islands. Common.

Masked Owl

Tyto novaehollandiae

Family: Barn Owls; Tytonidae

Identification: *350–500mm.* The world's largest barn owl with upperparts dark-brown to light chestnut with white speckling. Facial disc buff to chestnut with a darker margin. Females are considerably larger and darker than males.

Habits: Occurs singly or in pairs. A secretive bird, which roosts by day in a tree hollow, cave or dense foliage.

Voice: A rarely heard rasping hiss or screech.

Habitat: Forest, woodland, parks and nearby open country.

Breeding: Nests in a tree hollow or small cave. Eggs: 2–3.

Distribution: New Guinea, parts of Indonesia and Australia, including Tasmania, where it is widespread but rarely seen.

Tawny Frogmouth

Podargus strigoides

Family: Frogmouths; Podargidae

Identification: *330–460mm.* A large, strange, big-headed bird with large yellow eyes and a broad bill. The mostly grey plumage is intricately marked with black, buff and white mottles and streaks, providing superb camouflage while perched. Distinctive tuft of bristles above the bill. Female is browner.

Habits: Occurs singly, in pairs or small family parties. Roosts branch-like during the day. Nocturnal, often seen perched on fence-posts.

Voice: A persistent low 'oom–oom–oom' repeated slowly many times.

Habitat: Forests, woodland, parks and gardens with trees.

Breeding: Nest is a flimsy platform of twigs in a tree. Eggs: 2.

Distribution: Australia (including Tasmania). A widespread and common resident.

Australian Owlet-nightjar

Aegotheles cristatus

Family: Owlet-nightjars; Aegothelidae

Identification: *210–240mm*. A small owl-like bird with large black eyes and feeble pink legs. Short, broad bill. Overall plumage is grey with lighter barring. Earpatch grey or rufous. Underparts are paler grey.

Habits: Usually seen singly. Nocturnal, roosting by day in tree hollows. Flight is silent and direct with tail slightly fanned.

Voice: A penetrating, repetitive, high-pitched 'churr, churr, churr'.

Habitat: Forest woodland and scrub with mature old trees.

Breeding: Nests in a tree hollow lined with eucalypt leaves. Eggs: 3–4.

Distribution: New Guinea, Australia (including Tasmania). Uncommon to rare.

White-throated Needletail

Hirundapus caudacutus

Family: Swifts; Apodidae

Identification: *190–210mm.* Also known as Spine-tailed Swift. A large, sturdy, powerful swift with dark grey, almost black plumage. Throat and undertail are distinctively white. The short tail has protruding spines, which are not visible in flight.

Habits: Occurs in small parties or larger flocks, arriving during unsettled low-pressure systems. Typical flight is very fast with a series of rapid wingbeats followed by a glide.

Voice: A high-pitched twitter.

Habitat: Aerial.

Distribution: Breeds in Asia from Japan westwards through the Himalayas to Siberia. A common summer migrant to eastern Australia. Uncommon but regular visitor to Tasmania.

Azure Kingfisher

Alcedo azurea

Family: Kingfishers; Alcedinidae

Identification: *170–190mm*. A small, short-tailed kingfisher with an orange breast. Upperparts are a glossy rich azure blue with a buff-white patch on either side of the neck.

Habits: Occurs singly or in pairs. Usually seen perched on low branches over water. Dives into the water from its perch to catch fish.

Voice: A high-pitched, shrill distinctive 'peet-peet', often sounded during flight.

Habitat: Rivers and creeks with tree-lined banks.

Breeding: Nest is in a burrow dug into a riverside bank. Eggs: 5–7.

Distribution: New Guinea, northern and eastern Australia (including Tasmania). Uncommon resident.

Where to see: Gordon, Franklin, Pieman and Arthur rivers in western Tasmania.

Laughing Kookaburra

Dacelo novaeguineae

Family: Kingfishers; Alcedinidae

Identification: *420–470mm*. A familiar large kingfisher with a massive bill. Back and wings brown with scapulars edged in blue. Head is white with faint barrings. The white-edged tail is rufous with dark bars.

Habits: Occurs singly, in pairs or small family parties. Flight is direct and heavy. Tail is cocked upon alighting.

Voice: A well-known raucous laugh, usually uttered at dawn and dusk and repeated by other group members. Also 'kook-kook-kook' repeated.

Habitat: Open forest, woodland, parks and gardens.

Breeding: Nests in a tree hollow, often high. Eggs: 2–4.

Distribution: Mainland Australia. Introduced into Tasmania where it is now a common resident in the north and east.

Superb Lyrebird

Menura novaehollandiae

Family: Lyrebirds; Menuridae

Identification: Male to *1000mm*, female *750–850mm*. Dark-coloured ground bird often heard but rarely seen. Both sexes have a brown back and wings, grey underparts and head. Male's long tail has many filamentous plumes and two lyre-shaped outer tail feathers. The female lacks these.

Habits: Occurs singly or in pairs. Usually seen running along the forest floor.

Voice: Renowned for its fabulous, far-carrying mimicry of other birds, such as the Grey Shrike-thrush or Yellow-throated Honeyeater.

Habitat: Rainforests, wet forests and fern gullies.

Breeding: Males perform spectacular dancing displays on earthen mounds in the autumn–winter breeding season. Large, domed nest of sticks, fern fronds and bark is built on a bank, in a stump or on a tree-fern head. Eggs: 1.

Distribution: South-east mainland Australia and southern Tasmania where it was introduced near Mt Field NP in 1934 and Hastings Caves in 1945. A common and increasing resident, the range is extending west and north.

Where to see: Hastings Caves vicinity and Mt Field NP.

Wrens, Honeyeaters
& Robins

Superb Fairy-wren

Malurus cyaneus

Family: Australo-Papuan Wrens; Maluridae

Identification: *140mm*. An exquisite and extremely popular little bird. The male has a distinctive bright blue crown, ear coverts and upper back, and a glossy dark blue chest and throat. Wings are brown, belly is off-white and the long tail is dark blue. Female is brown overall. During winter, most males enter an eclipse plumage similar to that of the female.

Habits: Usually occurs in family groups or pairs. Hops and bounds energetically through undergrowth catching insects.

Voice: A musical trill.

Habitat: Open forest, woodland, scrub and gardens; in fact, almost anywhere with ground cover and open areas.

Breeding: Two or three broods may be produced each season due to cooperation by family members in raising the chicks. Nest is of grass, twigs and moss with a domed roof, built in shrubbery or tussock, close to ground level. Eggs: 3–4.

Distribution: South-east mainland Australia, including Tasmania and King and Flinders islands. Common resident.

Southern Emu-wren

Stipiturus malachurus

Family: Australo-Papuan Wrens; Maluridae

Identification: *160–200mm.* A small, shy wren with a long tail composed of six emu-like plumes. Upperparts are grey-rufous with dark brown streaks. The male has a lavender-blue eyebrow, throat and breast. Underparts are orange-buff.

Habits: Occurs in pairs or family parties that run across the ground; individuals sometimes climb exposed stems of grass tussocks or shrubs.

Voice: High-pitched and descending, similar to fairy-wrens. Also a soft chirp.

Habitat: Swampy heathland, bogs and button-grass plains.

Breeding: Nest is domed and built of woven grasses and sedge leaves, lined with fine grasses and feathers and placed close to the ground in a dense shrub or grass tussock. Eggs: 3.

Distribution: South-west Western Australia, south-east mainland, Tasmania. Uncommon resident.

Where to see: Melaleuca area (Port Davey), Strahan airport.

Spotted Pardalote

Pardalotus punctatus

Family: Pardalotes; Pardalotidae

Identification: *80–95mm*. A diminutive and jewel-like bird. The male has a black crown, wings and tail with distinctive white spots. The throat and undertail are yellow. Rump is red. Sides of the face are grey with white eyebrows. Female is duller and lacks the yellow throat.

Habits: Occurs singly, in pairs or small loose parties during winter.

Voice: A monotonous, high-pitched 'sleep baby'.

Habitat: Open forest, woodland, scrub, parks and gardens.

Breeding: Nest is domed and built of fine bark strips lined with soft grass at the end of a burrow dug into a bank or pile of earth. Eggs: 3–5.

Distribution: South-west, south-east and east mainland Australia, and Tasmania and Bass Strait islands. Common resident.

Forty-spotted Pardalote

Pardalotus quadragintus

Family: Pardalotes; Pardalotidae

Identification: *90–120mm*. A small, cryptic, dull bird. Overall plumage is greenish-olive. The darker wings have white spots and the sides of the face and under tail are pale yellow. Bill is short and dark.

Habits: Occurs singly, in pairs or small parties that feed on lerps in the foliage of eucalypts, particularly *Eucalyptus viminalis*.

Voice: A soft monotone double note, difficult to pick up.

Habitat: Dry eucalypt forest.

Breeding: Nest is built of fine strips of bark, usually in a tree hollow, a stump or sometimes in the ground. Eggs: 4.

Distribution: Endemic to Tasmania, where it occurs in a few eastern and southern localities. Rare and endangered resident.

Where to see: Maria Island. Almost any *Eucalyptus viminalis* woodland on north Bruny Island, especially McCrackens Gully and Dennes Hill. Also Peter Murrell Nature Reserve near Kingston.

133

Striated Pardalote

Pardalotus striatus

Family: Pardalotes; Pardalotidae

Identification: *90–115mm.* The plumage of this small bird varies considerably across Australia. The crown is striped black with a white streak behind the eye and a yellow patch between the eye and the bill. The wing primaries are edged white with a red spot at the base. The short black tail has a white tip. The flanks and throat are yellow.

Habits: Occurs singly, in pairs or in small family groups. Often feeds high in the foliage of eucalypts.

Voice: Double or treble notes. A repetitive 'pick-pick' or 'pick-id-up', which is a familiar sound of spring.

Habitat: Sclerophyll forest, open woodland and gardens.

Breeding: Domed nest made of fine grass rootlets and bark strips in a tree hollow, or at the end of a tunnel excavated in a bank or pile of soil. Eggs: 2–5.

Distribution: Several races are recognised across Australia. The nominate race occurs within Tasmania and on Bass Strait islands during the summer months. During winter it migrates to the south-east mainland. Common.

Tasmanian Scrubwren

Sericornis humilis

Family: Scrubwrens and Thornbills; Acanthizidae

Identification: *120–135mm.* A small, brown bird with cryptic plumage, which is variable. The eye is pale yellow with a black centre. The throat is pale grey to white with faint dark streaks. Pale white eyebrow. This bird was originally considered to be the same species as the White-browed Scrubwren, which is found on the mainland and has a more distinct facial pattern.

Habits: Occurs singly or in pairs and quickly hops under undergrowth or shrubs. Birds become tame in gardens.

Voice: A noisy scolding 'zizz' plus a repetitive clear 'see-choo, see-choo'.

Habitat: Forests, woodland and gardens and scrub with dense undergrowth.

Breeding: Nest is domed, an untidy, loosely built structure of fine twigs, rootlets, grasses and leaves, well hidden in a grass tussock, dense undergrowth usually close to the ground. Eggs: 2–3.

Distribution: Tasmania and Bass Strait islands. Common resident.

Where to see: Mt Wellington, Mt Field NP, Melaleuca (Port Davey).

Scrubtit

Acanthornis magnus

Family: Scrubwrens and Thornbills; Acanthizidae

Identification: *100mm.* A small, brown bird similar to a scrubwren except the eye is brown with a black centre and a whitish eye-ring. The ear coverts are grey. The long fine bill is curved. Throat and upperbreast are white. Flanks are buff-coloured.

Habits: Shy and easily missed; hops up trunks of trees similar to a treecreeper and creeps about under dense scrub.

Voice: Similar to scrubwren, a clear 'too-wee-too' and melodic whistling.

Habitat: Dense undergrowth of wet forests, fern-gullies and rainforests.

Breeding: The nest is domed and made of bark strips, fern fibre, grasses and moss. Often placed low in shrubbery or ferns. Eggs: 3–4.

Distribution: Endemic to Tasmania where it is locally uncommon.

Where to see: Mt Wellington, Mt Field NP.

Striated Fieldwren

Calamanthus fuliginosus

Family: Scrubwrens and Thornbills; Acanthizidae

Identification: *125–135mm.* A jaunty little bird that usually has its tail cocked. Greyish-brown upperparts are heavily streaked black. Yellow-buff underparts are also streaked. White eyestripe is tinged rufous towards the bill.

Habits: Occurs singly or in pairs. Frequently seen singing conspicuously from the top of a bush or fence post.

Voice: A musical churring twitter, 'whurr-whurr-chick-chick-chir-ee-ee'.

Habitat: Open areas with low ground cover, coastal heathland and button-grass plains.

Breeding: Nest is an untidy domed affair of plant stems and grasses low in a tussock or small bush. Eggs: 3–4.

Distribution: Coastal south-east mainland Tasmania. Uncommon resident.

Where to see: Melaleuca (Port Davey), Asbestos Range NP.

Brown Thornbill

Acanthiza pusilla

Family: Scrubwrens and Thornbills; Acanthizidae

Identification: *100mm*. A small, brown bird with a rufous-buff forehead with paler scallops. Upperparts olive-brown. Rump is cinnamon. Throat and breast are greyish with brown streaks. Flanks are buff-coloured. Eye is dark red.

Habits: Always active, it occurs singly, in pairs or frequently in family groups often mixed with other species. Feeds frequently on small insects in the canopy foliage.

Voice: Varied, including scrubwren-like scolding 'zizz', a short musical warbling and deep 'peee-oar'. An excellent mimic.

Habitat: Forests, woodland, scrub and gardens.

Breeding: Nest is an untidy domed affair of shredded bark, grass and some moss bound with spiderwebs, usually near the ground. Eggs: 3.

Distribution: Mainly coastal east and south-east mainland, Tasmania and Bass Strait islands. Common resident.

Tasmanian Thornbill

Acanthiza ewingii

Family: Scrubwrens and Thornbills; Acanthizidae

Identification: *100mm.* Similar to Brown Thornbill but the rich rufous-buff forehead has less obvious scallops and the bill is shorter. The throat and breast are whitish with grey streaks. Flanks and under-tail coverts are white.

Habits: Similar to Brown Thornbill but prefers wetter habitat.

Voice: Similar to Brown Thornbill.

Habitat: Wet sclerophyll forest, rainforest and closed wet scrub. Note preference for wetter, denser habitats than the previous species.

Breeding: Nest is neater than the Brown Thornbill's, often with more moss. Eggs: 3–4.

Distribution: Endemic to Tasmania and Bass Strait islands. Common.

Where to see: Mt Wellington, Mt Field NP, Maria Island and South Bruny Island.

Yellow-rumped Thornbill

Acanthiza chrysorrhoa

Family: Scrubwrens and Thornbills; Acanthizidae

Identification: *100–120mm*. The largest thornbill with the most distinctive markings. Upperparts are olive-green with a bright yellow rump. Tail is black with a white tip. Black forehead is flecked with a distinctive white eyestripe.

Habits: Occurs singly, in pairs or, during winter, in small parties that feed frequently on the ground.

Voice: A lively tinkling, often repeated. Flight call is a repeated 'chek-chek'.

Habitat: Open woodland, grasslands and gardens.

Breeding: Nest is a domed, untidy structure with a hidden entrance. Built of grasses, plant fibre and cobwebs lined with small feathers and down. Eggs: 3–4.

Distribution: Widespread across southern and eastern Australia, Tasmania and Bass Strait islands. Uncommon resident.

Yellow Wattlebird

Anthochaera paradoxa

Family: Honeyeaters; Meliphagidae

Identification: *380–480mm*. Australia's largest honeyeater has an overall grey-brown plumage with white streaks. The face, eyebrow and chin are white. The long, pendulous rich-yellow wattles attached to the ear are distinctive. The belly is also a rich yellow.

Habits: Occurs singly, in pairs or small family parties that gather at blossoming eucalypts and other shrubs. May become tame in gardens.

Voice: The guttural coughing gurgle is hardly musical and somewhat reminiscent of vomiting.

Habitat: Eucalypt forest and woodland, mountain shrubberies, scrub, orchards and gardens.

Breeding: The nest is a large untidy cup of twigs, bark and leaves lined with feathers and fine grasses. Placed high in foliage of shrub or tree. Eggs: 2–3.

Distribution: Endemic to Tasmania and King Island. Common.

Where to see: Bruny Island, Tinderbox, Maria Island and Forest Glen Tea Gardens.

Little Wattlebird

Anthochaera chrysoptera

Family: Honeyeaters; Meliphagidae

Identification: *270–320mm.* A dull brown honeyeater with no wattles. The overall grey-brown plumage is heavily streaked white. Note the pale face patch and deep ruby-red eye. A rufous wing patch is distinctive in flight.

Habits: An aggressive and vocal bird, it frequently occurs in parties that raid flowering banksias and other shrubs.

Voice: Males utter a loud rasping squawk and soft lilting squeaks; these squeaks are often repeated by females.

Habitat: Dry eucalypt forest, coastal scrub with banksias, also gardens.

Breeding: Nest is a loose, untidy cup of twigs, plant fibre and grasses lined with feathers and wool built up to 10m high in a fork of a bush or tree. Eggs: 1–3.

Distribution: South-west Western Australia and coastal south-east mainland. Common in coastal east and north Tasmania. Nomadic.

Noisy Miner

Manorina melanocephala

Family: Honeyeaters; Meliphagidae

Identification: *240–270mm.* A well-known, medium-sized greyish honeyeater with a distinctive head pattern. The black crown extends down behind the eye to the sides of the throat. Forehead is greyish white and there is a distinctive triangular bare patch of yellow skin behind the eye. The bill and legs are yellow.

Habits: Frequently occurs in small parties or larger flocks, which engage noisily in displays and aggression.

Voice: A piercing, high-pitched 'pwee-pwee-pwee' or 'teu-teu-teu' and other complex chuckles and twitters.

Habitat: Open forest with large eucalypts, scrub, orchards and gardens.

Breeding: Nest is a flimsy cup of twigs and grasses bound with cobwebs, lined with hair or wool in a fork of outer branches, up to 14m high. Often in loose colonies. Eggs: 2–4.

Distribution: Eastern and south-east mainland. Central and eastern lowlands of Tasmania. Common resident.

Yellow-throated Honeyeater

Lichenostomus flavicollis

Family: Honeyeaters; Meliphagidae

Identification: *190–210mm.* A distinctive, medium-small honeyeater with overall olive-green plumage with dark grey crown and face contrasting with the rich yellow chin and throat. Small yellow ear tuft. Deep ruby eye.

Habits: Usually occurs singly or sometimes as small family parties.

Voice: A loud, metallic 'tonk-tonk-tonk' repeated 3-4 times. Also aggressive churrs and 'chur-uk'.

Habitat: Wide variety, including wet and dry sclerophyll forests, alpine woodland, coastal heathland, parks and gardens but not rainforest.

Breeding: Nest is a deep cup of bark strips and leaves lined with plant fibre, wool and fur built low in a bush, tussock or bracken clump. Eggs: 2–3.

Distribution: Endemic to Tasmania and Bass Strait islands. Common.

Where to see: Mt Wellington, Bruny Island, Mt Field NP, Maria Island, Forest Glen Tea Gardens and many suburban gardens.

Strong-billed Honeyeater

Melithreptus validirostris

Family: Honeyeaters; Meliphagidae

Identification: *165–175mm.* Upperparts are olive-brown. The only honeyeater in Tasmania with a white nape band, which leads into a blue crescent over the eye. The head is otherwise black. Underparts are pale grey-brown; chin is black.

Habits: Occurs in pairs or small flocks. A highly specialised feeder, it works over the trunks and limbs of eucalypts while prising pieces of bark to search for insects.

Voice: A loud, sharp 'cheep-cheep'. Also a harsh churring.

Habitat: Wet and dry sclerophyll forests, particularly with dense undergrowth.

Breeding: Nest is a cup of grasses, shredded bark, fur and wool lined with wool, fur and fine grasses hung from outer branches of eucalypts or high in understorey. Eggs: 2–3.

Distribution: Endemic to Tasmania and Bass Strait islands. Common.

Where to see: Mt William, Weilangta Forest, South Bruny Island, Mt Field NP, Maria Island, Forest Glen Tea Gardens.

145

Black-headed Honeyeater

Melithreptus affinis

Family: Honeyeaters; Meliphagidae

Identification: *130–150mm.* A small honeyeater with an entirely black head and throat except for blue crescent over eye. Upperparts olive-green. Underparts off-white.

Habits: Often occurs in flocks sometimes mixed with Strong-billed Honeyeaters. Aggressive and active.

Voice: A high-pitched double-noted whistle. Also a harsh 'cherp-cherp'.

Habitat: Wet and dry sclerophyll forests but not rainforests. Also orchards and gardens.

Breeding: Similar to the Strong-billed Honeyeater. Nest is a suspended cup in the outer branches of eucalypts. Eggs: 2–3.

Distribution: Endemic to Tasmania, mainly in the north and east, and Bass Strait islands. Common.

Where to see: Mt Wellington, Bruny Island, Mt Field NP, Maria Island, Forest Glen Tea Gardens, Weilangta Forest.

Crescent Honeyeater

Phylidonyris pyrrhoptera

Family: Honeyeaters; Meliphagidae

Identification: *140–160mm.* A dark grey honeyeater with a distinctive yellow panel on each wing. Eyebrow is black-and-white. A broad black crescent edged in white runs down the sides of the breast. Eye is deep ruby. Female is an overall dull olive-brown.

Habits: An altitudinal migrant moving to the lowlands during autumn. Occurs singly or in pairs, feeding primarily on nectar.

Voice: A loud metallic 'egypt', a typical Tasmanian bush sound; also melodic twittering.

Habitat: Rainforest, wet and dry sclerophyll forest, alpine woodland, coastal heathland and gardens.

Breeding: Nest is a deep cup of shredded bark, twigs and cobwebs lined with fine grass or hair in low bush or fern clump. Eggs: 2–3.

Distribution: South-east mainland, Tasmania and Bass Strait islands. Common but nomadic.

Where to see: Melaleuca (Port Davey), Mt Wellington, Weilangta Forest.

New Holland Honeyeater

Phylidonyris novaehollandiae

Family: Honeyeaters; Meliphagidae

Identification: *165–175mm.* A familiar honeyeater with plumage boldly streaked black-and-white with a distinctive yellow wing patch. White eyebrow and ear coverts. Iris is white. Black tail has a yellow edge to the outer tail feathers and a white tip.

Habits: Occurs singly, in pairs or in small parties gathering in prime blossoming habitat to feed on nectar or hawk for insects. Frequently perches on exposed branches or shrubs.

Voice: A harsh 'jick' when feeding. Alarm call is a rapid squeaking whistle. A high-pitched whistling 'phseet' called from a perch or during song flight.

Habitat: Dry sclerophyll forest, tea-tree scrub, coastal heathland and gardens.

Breeding: Nest is a large cup of woven twigs, grass and bark fibre usually in leafy fork of low shrub or tree. Eggs: 1–3.

Distribution: South-west Western Australia, south-east mainland, Tasmania and Bass Strait islands. Widespread and common resident.

Tawny-crowned Honeyeater

Phylidonyris melanops

Family: Honeyeaters; Meliphagidae

Identification: *145–170mm.* A slender, attractive pale brown honeyeater with tawny coloured crown. Eyebrow and chin are white. A black sash extends from the bill through the eye down the sides of the breast. Underparts are dull white.

Habits: Occurs singly, in pairs or small loose parties during winter. Spectacular song flights during spring identify their breeding territories.

Voice: A high-pitched ascending, fluted 'a-peer-peer-pee-pee-pee', often followed by trilling whistles uttered from the perch or during song-flight.

Habitat: Coastal heathland and grass trees.

Breeding: Nest is a deep cup of bark strips and grass lined with soft grass strips and wool placed in low shrub or on the ground. Eggs: 2–3.

Distribution: South-west Western Australia, south-east mainland, Tasmania and Bass Strait islands. Common resident within a restricted habitat.

Where to see: South Bruny Island, heathland near Strahan, Waterhouse Conservation Area.

Eastern Spinebill

Acanthorhynchus tenuirostris

Family: Honeyeaters; Meliphagidae

Identification: *145–160mm.* A small, active honeyeater with a long, fine decurved bill. Male has a black crown that extends down as a crescent either side of a white breast. There is a black and rufous patch in the centre of the white throat. Upper back and nape are rufous-buff. Wings are metallic blue-grey. Female is less colourful than the male.

Habits: Occurs singly or in pairs gathering at blossom, where it hovers like a hummingbird.

Voice: A clear, rapid piping whistle; also twittering whistle during song-flight.

Habitat: Sclerophyll forest, rainforest, scrub and gardens.

Breeding: Nest is a small cup of grasses, hair and moss lined with feathers and attached to a fork of small twigs in a shrub or tree. Eggs: 2–3.

Distribution: Eastern, south-east mainland and Tasmania. Rare or almost non-existent on Bass Strait islands. Common and nomadic.

White-fronted Chat

Epthianura albifrons

Family: Scrubwrens and Thornbills; Acanthizidae

Identification: *110–125mm*. The male is very distinctive with a bold white forehead, face and underparts contrasting with a jet-black band forming a collar from the nape, around the neck and breast. The eye is pinky-orange. The upperparts are grey with dark brown wings. The female is browner above with a brown breast band and lacks the white face of the male.

Habits: Occurs singly, in pairs or in small parties that feed on or close to the ground. Frequently perches on prominent bushes or fence posts. Flight is characteristic, with flitting of wings.

Voice: A soft metallic 'tang' often repeated.

Habitat: Open areas with low ground cover, often wet or saline. More common in coastal areas of Tasmania. It has adapted to areas of gorse.

Breeding: Nest is a deep cup of small twigs and grasses built in a shrub or tussock, usually close to the ground. Eggs: 3–4.

Distribution: Southern Australia, Tasmania, Bass Strait islands. Common.

Where to see: Any coastal areas of Tasmania.

Scarlet Robin

Petroica multicolor

Family: Flycatchers, Whistlers and Thrushes; Muscicapidae

Identification: *120–130mm.* A small, plump old-world flycatcher. Male has scarlet breast with black head, throat, back and tail. Bold white forehead and distinctive wing bar. Female is brownish overall with rose-washed breast and white forehead.

Habits: Occurs singly or in pairs.

Voice: Male has a pretty territorial song often repeated.

Habitat: Dry woodland and gardens, also more open country.

Breeding: Nest is a cup of grass, bark strips and moss, decorated with spiders webs in a tree. Eggs: 3.

Distribution: Tasmania and south-east and south-west mainland. Common.

Flame Robin

Petroica phoenicea

Family: Flycatchers, Thrushes and Whistlers; Muscicapidae

Identification: *125–135mm*. A strikingly coloured robin, the male has dark-grey upperparts contrasting with brilliant orange-red breast and belly. Small white forehead patch and bold white wing bar. Female has overall buff-brown upperparts with paler grey-brown underparts.

Habits: Occurs singly or in pairs. Frequently flicks wings and tail when perched.

Voice: Males song is a sweet lilting piping; louder than the Scarlet Robin.

Habitat: Prefers more open country than other robins, favouring dry forest and savannah woodland from coastal to sub-alpine.

Breeding: Nest is a neat cup of green moss, bark strips and cobwebs, decorated with lichen, in a fork of a bush or tree in dense undergrowth. Eggs: 3–4.

Distribution: South-east mainland, Tasmania and Bass Strait islands. Part-migratory and common.

Where to see: Maria Island, Bruny Island.

Pink Robin

Petroica rodinogaster

Family: Flycatchers, Thrushes and Whistlers; Muscicapidae

Identification: *115–130mm*. A small, dark robin, which is quiet and rarely seen. Male has uniformly sooty-brown upperparts and bib. Breast and belly is a dusky, rose-pink. Female has olive-brown upperparts with pale brown to buff underparts sometimes with a pale pink wash.

Habits: Occurs singly or in pairs. Feeds on the ground in undergrowth.

Voice: The males' song is a soft irregular warbling. Both sexes utter a sharp 'tick', which is reminiscent of a twig snapping.

Habitat: Wet forests, rainforests and coastal tea-tree scrub. Breeds in densely vegetated gullies or tea-tree thickets.

Breeding: Nest is a neat cup of green moss, bark strips and cobwebs and is decorated with lichen, in a fork of a tree in dense undergrowth. Eggs: 3–4.

Distribution: Far south-east mainland, Tasmania and Bass Strait islands. Uncommon and nomadic.

Where to see: South Bruny Island, Melaleuca (Port Davey), Mt Wellington, Weilangta Forest.

Dusky Robin

Melanodryas vittata

Family: Flycatchers, Thrushes and Whistlers: Muscicapidae

Identification: *160–170mm*. An overall plain brown robin. Upperparts are dark-olive brown with a narrow white shoulder to the wing. Immatures are attractively streaked and mottled.

Habits: Occurs singly, in pairs or small family parties. Feeds by perching silently on twigs or stumps before flying to the ground to feed on insects.

Voice: A soft double whistle, repeated monotonously. Also a brighter 'choo-wee-er'.

Habitat: Open woodland, forest edges, scrub and gardens.

Breeding: Nest is a cup of bark strips and grass concealed in the fork of a tree or cavity in a stump. Eggs: 3–4.

Distribution: Endemic to Tasmania and Bass Strait islands. Common.

Where to see: Bruny Island, Maria Island, Forest Glen Tea Gardens, Melaleuca (Port Davey).

Spotted Quail-thrush

Cinclosoma punctatum

Family: Quail Thrushes and Whipbirds; Orthonychidae

Identification: *260–280mm*. Tasmania's only quail-thrush is an attractively marked bird. The male has a black face with bold white eyebrows and a white patch each side of the throat. The neck and breast are grey. Upperparts are grey-brown with bold black streaks. Female is duller.

Habits: Occurs in pairs or small family parties that feed on the forest floor. Wary and elusive.

Voice: A very high-pitched, long, drawn-out repeated whistle. The song, uttered from a perch, consists of 10–12 soft but fluty double whistles.

Habitat: Dry sclerophyll forest and scrub with stony ridges and outcrops; prefers a forest floor covered with leaf litter and fallen branches.

Breeding: Nest is a depression in the ground lined with leaves, grass and bark to form a cup; near a rock, tree stump or grass tussock. Eggs: 2–3.

Distribution: South-east mainland and Tasmania. Uncommon and local resident.

Where to see: The Hazards Freycinet NP.

Whistlers, Woodswallows, Crows & Finches

Olive Whistler

Pachycephala olivacea

Family: Flycatchers, Thrushes and Whistlers; Muscicapidae

Identification: *200–215mm.* An overall olive-brown bird with a dark grey head and off-white throat with dark barrings. Female is duller with more olive-brown head.

Habits: Occurs solitary or in pairs during breeding.

Voice: Low, sweet whistle. Usually located by the 'too-wee-e-chow' call with the final syllable like a whipcrack similar to the mainland Eastern Whipbird.

Habitat: Dense wet forests, tea-tree forests, coastal heath and scrub, thickly vegetated gardens.

Breeding: Nest is a large cup of twigs, bark and leaves in bush. Eggs: 2–3.

Distribution: South-east mainland, Tasmania and Bass Strait islands. Common though elusive resident.

Where to see: South Bruny Island, Melaleuca (Port Davey), Mt Wellington.

Golden Whistler

Pachycephala pectoralis

Family: Flycatchers, Thrushes and Whistlers; Muscicapidae

Identification: *160–180mm.* The male is a distinctive bird with a black head that extends around the breast in a band, white throat and a rich yellow nape extending into a collar and yellow underparts. Back and wings are olive-green. Female is mid-grey with olive-wash on the upperparts.

Habits: Occurs singly, usually in pairs during breeding season. Males display and call during spring.

Voice: Loud, melodious clear whistles often ending in a sharp crack. Similar to other whistlers, the males often call following a sudden loud noise such as thunder.

Habitat: Wet sclerophyll forests, rainforests, orchards and well-vegetated gardens.

Breeding: Nest is a rough cup of bark strips, plant stems, grass, twigs and cobwebs. Eggs: 2–3.

Distribution: South-west Western Australia, south-east and east mainland, Tasmania and Bass Strait islands. Common resident.

Grey Shrike-thrush

Colluricincla harmonica

Family: Flycatchers, Thrushes and Whistlers; Muscicapidae

Identification: *220–260mm.* An overall grey, thrush-sized bird. Back and wings olive-grey to olive-brown. White stripe from eye to bill. Female is similar to male but with a white eye-ring.

Habits: Occurs singly, in pairs or sometimes small families following breeding. Frequently seen foraging for insects along logs, branches and ground litter.

Voice: An incredibly rich and melodious song, typically 'jock-widd-ee' or similar, with a strongly ascending last syllable.

Habitat: All types of forest and woodland, scrub, parks and gardens. Common and widespread.

Breeding: Nest is a large, untidy cup of bark strips, rootlets and grass lined with fine rootlets placed in a hollow of a stump, vine on a wall, tree fork or in a dense shrub. Eggs: 3–4.

Distribution: Australia-wide, Tasmania and Bass Strait islands. Common.

Satin Flycatcher

Myiagra cyanoleuca

Family: Flycatchers, Thrushes and Whistlers; Muscicapidae

Identification: *160–180mm*. Male is distinctive with the head, wings, back, tail, throat and upperbreast a glossy blue-black, contrasting strongly with the white underparts. Female is dusky blue-grey above, with a rich buff throat and upper breast, and white underparts.

Habits: Occurs singly or in pairs, flitting among branches of canopy while rapidly quivering the tail.

Voice: A strident guttural 'zurrp' repeated often. Also a far carrying, clear double-noted whistle 'tchoo-ee, tcho-ee' or 'pewit-pewit-pewit'.

Habitat: Sclerophyll forest.

Breeding: Nest is a neat cup of grass and fine shredded bark coated with cobwebs and sometimes lichen, usually placed at a fork of a dead branch high in a tree. Eggs: 2–3.

Distribution: Eastern mainland, Tasmania and Bass Strait islands. A common summer migrant.

Where to see: South Bruny Island, Waterworks Reserve-Hobart.

Grey Fantail

Rhipidura fuliginosa

Family: Flycatchers, Thrushes and Whistlers; Muscicapidae

Identification: *150–170mm*. The Tasmanian race is the darkest of the five races. Upperparts are dark grey with a white eyebrow, a white mark behind the eye and white throat. The long fan-shaped tail is dark grey with white tip and outer tail feathers. Dark sooty breast band with a creamy buff belly.

Habits: Occurs singly, in pairs or small parties during winter. Colloquially known as 'Cranky Fans' due to their highly active habits of twisting and turning in flight with the tail fanned and wings drooping.

Voice: A single or double 'dick', often repeated, which develops into a thin squeaky ascending little song.

Habitat: Prefers sclerophyll forest, tea-tree lined creeks and coastal scrub.

Breeding: Nest is a small neat cup of plant fibre bound with cobwebs placed on a thin fork of shrub or tree. Eggs: 2–3.

Distribution: Australia-wide, including Tasmania and Bass Strait islands. A common summer migrant, although a few may overwinter.

Black-faced Cuckoo-shrike

Coracina novaehollandiae

Family: Cuckoo-Shrikes; Campephagidae

Identification: *310–350mm*. A familiar and distinctive light-grey bird with a black face and throat. The black flight feathers have pale edges. Long grey tail is edged black. Sexes are similar.

Habits: Occurs singly, in pairs or small flocks. Distinctive undulating flight. They characteristically refold the wings several times when alighting.

Voice: A metallic, rolling, churring note. Also a higher 'chereer-chereer-chereer' uttered during flight or display.

Habitat: Open forest and woodland, scrub, orchards and gardens.

Breeding: Nest is a small neat saucer built of small twigs and shredded bark bound with cobwebs and placed on a branch or fork of tree at height. Eggs: 2–3.

Distribution: Australia-wide, including Tasmania and Bass Strait islands. A common summer migrant, although some birds may overwinter.

White-browed Woodswallow

Artamus superciliosus

Family: Woodswallows; Artamidae

Identification: *200mm*. Male is most attractive with blue-grey upperparts, throat and upper breast. Underparts are rich chestnut. Bold white stripe over the eye is distinctive. Tail has a white tip. Female is paler above with less-distinct white eyebrows.

Habits: Occurs often in small groups; nomadic. Frequently seen perched atop bushes or on dead branches, or soaring overhead.

Voice: A musical 'chap chap'. Song is quiet with some mimicry. Also harsh scolding.

Habitat: Open woodland, scrub and farmland.

Breeding: Nest is a flimsy shallow saucer of grass and small twigs lined with rootlets, placed in a fork of tree or in a jagged stump. Eggs: 2–3.

Distribution: Inland and east Australia. Rare in Tasmania where breeding has occurred sporadically including 1972, 1982 and 1997 in the north of the State.

Where to see: Northern Tasmania, particularly Cape Portland.

Dusky Woodswallow

Artamus cyanopterus

Family: Woodswallows; Artamidae

Identification: *170–180mm.* An overall smoky-brown bird with slate-coloured wings and white edges to the outer primaries. The black tail has a white tip. The blue-grey bill has a black tip and the eye is dark brown. In flight, note the contrast between the dark body and white leading edge of the wing. Sexes are similar.

Habits: Occurs singly, in pairs or small to medium flocks.

Voice: A pleasant, animated collection of chirrups, 'chirp-chirp', 'peert-peert' in flight or at rest. Also a harsh chattering while harassing larger birds.

Habitat: Sclerophyll forest and woodland, coastal scrub and wooded farmland.

Breeding: Often nests in loose colonies. Nest is an untidy basket of twigs, grasses and rootlets lined with fine plant stems or rootlets; placed in a fork of a branch, an open tree cavity or behind a piece of bark of tree. Eggs: 3–4.

Distribution: South-west, south-east and east mainland, Tasmania and Bass Strait islands. A common summer migrant.

Grey Butcherbird

Cracticus torquatus

Family: Butcherbirds and Currawongs; Cracticidae

Identification: *250–300mm.* A familiar bird with grey upperparts, a black head and an incomplete white collar. The blue-grey bill has a finely hooked black tip. The black wing has a white streak on the secondaries. Underparts are pale grey. Female has a slightly browner head than the male.

Habits: Occurs singly, in pairs or small family groups. Bold yet wary, it waits watchfully on a perch before darting onto prey such as insects, small birds or reptiles. Becomes tame in gardens.

Voice: A beautiful, melodic piping and warbling, far-carrying, often in duet. A softer sub-song includes some mimicry.

Habitat: Sclerophyll forests, coastal scrub, wooded farmland and gardens.

Breeding: Nest is an untidy cup of rootlets and twigs lined with fine rootlets and grasses; placed in a shrubby tree fork. Eggs: 3–5.

Distribution: Australia-wide, except the centre and Cape York. Tasmania. A common resident.

Australian Magpie

Gymnorhina tibicen

Family: Butcherbirds and Currawongs; Cracticidae

Identification: *380–440mm.* A large, familiar, black-and-white bird that is essentially a ground-feeding butcherbird. The head and underparts are jet-black. The black wings have a bold white shoulder patch. The nape, back and rump are all white. Female has the nape and upper back flecked grey. Immatures are grey-brown instead of black.

Habits: Occurs singly, in pairs or small family parties. Becomes tame in campgrounds, picnic areas or gardens.

Voice: A rich, mellow flute-like carolling, uttered particularly at dawn and often in a duet. Also a short, harsh shout and caw in alarm.

Habitat: Open forest, woodland, wooded farmland, parks and gardens.

Breeding: Nest is an untidy bowl of sticks lined with hair, wool or grass built in the outer branches of tree. Eggs: 2–4.

Distribution: Widespread across mainland Australia and Tasmania. Introduced to King and Flinders islands. A common resident.

Black Currawong

Strepera fuliginosa

Family: Butcherbirds and Currawongs; Cracticidae

Identification: *470–490mm*. An all-black bird except for a white tip to the tail primaries and small, white patch in the wing. Eye is bright-yellow.

Habits: Occurs singly, in pairs or flocks of up to 50 in winter. Typical swooping and floating flight of currawongs. Tame near campgrounds.

Voice: Distinctive, loud rolling 'kar-week-week-kar'. Also softer squeaks and mewings.

Habitat: Mainly sub-alpine forest and woodland, sometimes moving to lower ground during winter. Occurs in open woodland and coastal scrub on Bass Strait islands.

Breeding: Nest is a large bowl of sticks lined with fine roots and grasses built in an upright fork of a tree. Eggs: 2–4.

Distribution: Endemic to Tasmania where it is common and altitudinally nomadic.

Where to see: Cradle Mountain–Lake St Clair NP, Mt Wellington, Mt Field NP, Maria Island.

Grey Currawong
Strepera versicolor

Family: Butcherbirds and Currawongs; Cracticidae

Identification: *450–520mm*. Large, dark grey bird with a white wing patch, undertail coverts and tip to tail. The eye is bright yellow. Sexes are similar.

Habits: Occurs singly, in pairs, family parties or larger flocks during winter.

Voice: A distinctive ringing 'clink-clank' gives it the local name of Clinking Currawong.

Habitat: Sclerophyll forest, woodland, coastal scrub and orchards; also found in some gardens.

Breeding: Nest is a large, shallow cup of sticks lined with rootlets and grass; built high in the foliage of a tree. Eggs: 2–4.

Distribution: South-west Western Australia, central Australia, south-east mainland, Tasmania. Common and nomadic.

Forest Raven

Corvus tasmanicus

Family: Crows; Corvidae

Identification: *520–540mm.* The largest of all ravens is an all-black bird with a white eye. Bill is large and prominent and the tail short. Sexes are similar.

Habits: Occurs singly, in pairs or in large flocks during winter. Frequently seen foraging for carrion alongside roads.

Voice: A very deep bass 'korr-korr-korr' with last note drawn out.

Habitat: Wide range of habitats from alpine moorland and forests to sclerophyll woodland, coastal scrub, beaches, roadsides and gardens.

Breeding: Nest is a large basket of sticks lined with shredded bark and wool; built high in a fork of a tree. Eggs: 4.

Distribution: Scattered localised populations of the south-east mainland and some Bass Strait islands. Common and nomadic in Tasmania.

Little Raven

Corvus mellori

Family: Crows; Corvidae

Identification: *480–500mm.* An all-black raven, slightly smaller than Forest Raven and having a smaller bill. Eye is white. Sexes are similar.

Habits: Occurs singly, in pairs or larger flocks.

Voice: A series of quick, deep somewhat guttural barks.

Habitat: Occurs throughout a wide range of habitats including open woodland, scrub and pastoral areas.

Breeding: Nest is a bulky basket of sticks lined with shredded bark and wool; placed high in the branches of a tree. Eggs: 4–5.

Distribution: South-east mainland, King Island and northern Tasmania. Common and nomadic visitor to King Island. Rarely seen on the north coast of Tasmania.

Skylark

Alauda arvensis

Family: Larks; Alaudidae

Identification: *170–190mm.* A familiar and melodious songster with upperparts pale brown covered in darker streaks. Crown feathers are raised in a small, pale brown crest. Eyebrow is pale buff. The longish tail is slightly forked with white edges. The breast is cream-buff and heavily streaked darker brown. The sexes are similar although the male is slightly larger.

Habits: Most distinctive is the male's habit of hovering during the song flight, which can last for several minutes while ascending to great heights. Occurs singly, in pairs or small loose parties.

Voice: One of the world's great avian songsters, the Skylark has had many songs written about it. The song consists of a beautiful high-pitched warbling sustained for several minutes.

Breeding: Nest is a cup of grass built on the ground, usually under a small tussock. Eggs: 3–5.

Distribution: Introduced into mainland Australia and Tasmania during the mid-1800s. Common and nomadic resident.

Richard's Pipit

Anthus novaeseelandiae

Family: Pipits and Wagtails; Motacillidae

Identification: *170–185mm.* A small, brown bird with buff upperparts covered in darker mottles. Note the two dark stripes on the cheek and pale eyebrow stripe. Underparts are pale buff with dark brown streaks.

Habits: Occurs singly or in pairs. Often seen walking or running jerkily with frequent stops to perch on stones.

Voice: A thin brisk 'tswee' or sparrow-like chirrup.

Habitat: Open country, native grasslands, wet heath and pastures.

Breeding: Nest is a deep cup of grasses built in a depression in the ground, usually under a tussock. Eggs: 2–4.

Distribution: Widespread throughout the Australian mainland, Tasmania and Bass Strait islands. Common and nomadic.

House Sparrow

Passer domesticus

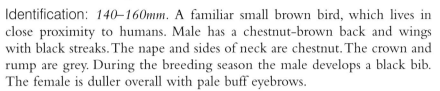

Family: Old World Sparrows; Passeridae

Identification: *140–160mm.* A familiar small brown bird, which lives in close proximity to humans. Male has a chestnut-brown back and wings with black streaks. The nape and sides of neck are chestnut. The crown and rump are grey. During the breeding season the male develops a black bib. The female is duller overall with pale buff eyebrows.

Habits: Occurs singly, in pairs or large flocks. Usually very sociable. A perky and sometimes tame bird, it feeds on insects and seeds on the ground. Hops on the ground and dust bathes.

Voice: A persistent 'chirp' and a variety of tiny rattles and chirrupings.

Habitat: Usually found near towns, villages, farm buildings and farmland.

Breeding: Nest is an untidy dome of dry grass, rags or paper lined with feathers; built in a crevice in a building or a tree hollow. Eggs: 4–6.

Distribution: Native of Europe and Asia. Introduced to mainland Australia and Tasmania during the 1860s and now widespread. Common resident.

Beautiful Firetail

Stagonopleura bella

Family: Australian Grass-finches; Ploceidae

Identification: *115–125mm*. A tubby, dark finch with a scarlet bill and rump. Black mask around a pale blue eye-ring. The upperparts are dark grey-brown, finely barred with black. The underparts are finely barred black-and-white. The plumage of breeding males darkens and the eye-ring becomes bluer. Sexes are similar.

Habits: Occurs singly, in pairs or small parties. Usually feeds on the ground near cover. Red rump most distinctive in flight.

Voice: A simple penetrating whistle 'weee'; also a drawn out 'pee-you, pee-you'.

Habitat: Varied, from sclerophyll woodland, tea-tree thickets and scrub, particularly coastal although range also extends into mountains.

Breeding: Nest is an untidy dome of grass stems and twigs built with an entrance spout in the foliage of a dense shrub, such as tea-tree. Eggs: 4–7.

Distribution: Coastal south-east mainland, Tasmania and Bass Strait islands.

Where to see: Melaleuca (Port Davey), South Bruny Island and heathland near Strahan, Ferntree area, Mt Wellington.

European Greenfinch

Carduelis chloris

Family: Finches; Fringillidae

Identification: *140–160mm.* A dull greenish-yellow finch with a short stubby pale horn-coloured bill. Wings are grey with yellow wing-bar. Tail is dark grey and forked. Female is duller and browner than male. Note yellow wing patches in flight.

Habits: Occurs singly, in pairs or small sociable flocks during winter. Feeds on the ground on seeds, buds or insects.

Voice: On take-off, a musical alarm 'cheu-cheu-cheu-cheu'. Also a canary-like trilling and twittering song.

Habitat: Open woodland, grasslands, paddocks orchards gardens and coastal scrub. Commonly associated with introduced conifers.

Breeding: Nest is a bulky cup of fine twigs and soft fibre, lined with plant down, feathers and hair and built in the foliage of a shrub or exotic tree such as pine. Eggs: 4–6.

Distribution: Coastal south-east mainland and lowlands of Tasmania. Common and nomadic. Introduced to Tasmania.

European Goldfinch

Carduelis carduelis

Family: Finches; Fringillidae

Identification: *125–135mm.* An attractive pale brown finch with a deep-red face surrounded by a broad white patch and black crown. Bill is a pale horn colour. Black wings have distinctive broad yellow wing-bars and white 'windows' in the primaries. Underparts are off-white with buff sides to breast and belly. Sexes are similar.

Habits: Occurs singly, in pairs or often in small winter flocks that feed on the ground on seeds, flowering grasses or seeding thistles.

Voice: A repeated, high-pitched tinkling, often during flight. Also a pretty song, 'twee-delit, twee-delit' or 'tsee-dit'.

Habitat: Wastelands with weeds, grasslands, paddocks, gardens.

Breeding: Nest is a neat cup of soft fibres, rootlets and grass, lined with fur or plant down and often decorated with lichens. Built in the ends of branches of a shrub or tree. Eggs: 4–6.

Distribution: Introduced to south-east mainland and Tasmania during 1880s. Common and nomadic.

Welcome Swallow

Hirundo neoxena

Family: Swallows and Martins; Hirundinidae

Identification: *145–155mm*. The familiar swallow of Australia. The forehead, face and throat are russet except for black lores. Upperparts are glossy blue-black with browner wings. Underparts are pale buff to off-white. The long tail is deeply forked. Sexes are similar.

Habits: Occurs singly, in pairs or larger flocks following breeding.

Voice: Contact call is a single sharp 'chep' usually heard in flight. Song is a well-known warbling twitter usually uttered from a perch.

Habitat: It is widespread in open country particularly near man-made structures such as farm buildings, bridges and verandahs; also frequents lagoons, rivers and swamps.

Breeding: Nest is a cup of mud pellets held together with grass and lined with feathers; usually fastened to shelf or beam under a verandah or attached to a vertical wall, under a bridge or in a tree hollow. Eggs: 3–6.

Distribution: Southern and eastern Australia, Tasmania and Bass Strait islands. A common summer migrant.

Tree Martin

Hirundo nigricans

Family: Swallows and Martins; Hirundinidae

Identification: *125–135mm.* A dark-coloured martin with glossy blue-black upper back and crown. Wings are dusky brown and the rump is white. Forehead is buff and the underparts are off-white. Throat is finely streaked grey. Tail has a square end. Sexes are similar.

Habits: A sociable bird, frequently seen flying around large eucalypts.

Voice: Animated twittering and a short 'drrt-drrt'.

Habitat: Wooded areas especially with mature eucalypts, often near water.

Breeding: Nest is usually in a tree hollow or sometimes a hole in a building or cliff. Nest chamber is lined with grass and leaves. Nests are in loose colonies, sometimes with several pairs using a single entrance. Eggs: 3–5.

Distribution: Widespread in suitable habitat across Australia, Tasmania and Bass Strait islands. A common summer migrant.

179

Clamorous Reed-Warbler

Acrocephalus stentoreus

Family: Old World Warblers; Sylviidae

Identification: *150–170mm.* The familiar songster of reedbeds. Upperparts and head are warm olive-brown with pale buff eyebrows. Flanks are cinnamon-buff. Sexes are similar.

Habits: Occurs singly and in pairs. Usually unobtrusive remaining hidden in dense reedbeds except during the breeding season, when males cling high on a reed stem to sing.

Voice: The song is a loud, rich and persistent 'cutch-cutch-cutch, deet-deet-deet, cotchy-cotchy-cotchy', also a scolding rattle and sharp 'tchut' in alarm.

Habitat: Reedbeds and other dense vegetation near fresh water, such as willows.

Breeding: Nest is a deep cup of woven reeds lined with fine grass and attached to upright reed stems. Eggs: 3–4.

Distribution: Widespread in suitable habitat of mainland Australia. In Tasmania it is restricted to the north of the State. An uncommon summer migrant.

Where to see: Tamar Wetlands, Gould's Lagoon.

Little Grassbird

Megalurus gramineus

Family: Old World Warblers; Sylviidae

Identification: *13,5–140mm.* A common but rarely seen small, brown bird. Upperparts are grey-brown to warm olive-brown with heavy dark streaks. Crown is more tawny and eyebrow is pale buff. Underparts are pale buff with fine dusky spots and streaks. The bill and eyes are brown. The long tapered tail is often carried cocked. Sexes are similar.

Habits: Unobtrusive and cryptic. Occurs singly or in pairs. Hops and runs in cover while searching for insects, aquatic molluscs and spiders.

Voice: A mournful, three-syllable whistle 'pe-peeee-peeee'. Also a rapid, scolding rattle.

Habitat: Reedbeds and dense vegetation near freshwater and tidal marshes.

Breeding: Nest is a deep, untidy cup of reeds, aquatic leaves and grass, sometimes partly domed, lined with feathers; placed in clumps of reeds, rushes or tussock. Eggs: 3–5.

Distribution: South-west Western Australia, south-east mainland, Tasmania and Bass Strait islands. Uncommon resident.

Where to see: Gould's Lagoon.

Golden-headed Cisticola

Cisticola exilis

Family: Old World Warblers; Silviidae

Identification: *95–115mm.* A small, active bird, which is rarely seen. Male in breeding plumage has plain golden-buff head. Upperparts are buff, heavily streaked black. Underparts are cream to rufous-buff. The short tail is dusky buff with a dark sub-terminal band. Non-breeding male and female are similar, with blackish streaks on a buff crown.

Habits: Occurs singly, in pairs or loose parties. Breeding males call from exposed perches and then launch into jerky song flights.

Voice: Breeding males call incessantly with grating, metallic insect-like 'bzzt' followed by several loud 'plink-plinks'.

Habitat: Tall grass and swampy grassland, usually near water.

Breeding: Nest is a small, rounded dome of fine grass and plant down with growing leaves stitched onto the outside; built in low vegetation, rushes or a tussock. Eggs: 3–4.

Distribution: Coastal and sub-coastal mainland Australia from north-west, north, east and south-east. Occurs regularly on King Island.

Silvereye

Zosterops lateralis

Family: White-eyes; Zosteropidae

Identification: *105–125mm*. The only small olive-green bird in Tasmania with a distinctive white eye-ring. Upperparts are olive-green with a grey back. Throat and breast are grey, flanks are rich chestnut to dull buff and under tail coverts are off white. Female is usually paler.

Habits: Occurs singly, in pairs, small parties or larger flocks. Frequently visits fruit trees, bird tables and nectar feeders.

Voice: Song is a loud mixture or trill, and warbles are uttered by the male. Also a thin, drawn-out 'psee' in contact and 'wee-wee-ee-ee-ee-' in alarm.

Habitat: Wide range, including forest, scrub, orchards and gardens.

Breeding: Nest is a beautiful and neat cup of fine grasses, moss and horse-hair bound with cobwebs and suspended between small branches in outer foliage of shrub or low tree. Eggs: 2–4.

Distribution: Several races are found on the southern and eastern mainland. Common in Tasmania and Bass Strait islands. Most birds migrate north during winter.

Bassian Thrush

Zoothera lunulata

Family: Flycatchers, Thrushes and Whistlers; Muscicapidae

Identification: *260–290mm*. Tasmania's only true thrush has grey-brown to coppery brown upperparts with feathers edged with black to give a scaly appearance. Whitish below with russet wash on breast. Feathers of breast, throat and flanks are edged in black scallops. Eye is dark brown. Sexes are similar although the female is slightly smaller than the male.

Habits: Occurs singly or in pairs. Quiet and unobtrusive, spending much time foraging on the forest floor for worms, insects and fallen fruit.

Voice: A mostly silent bird. Sometimes utters a thin 'seep' for contact. Also two clear, descending whistles are sung by the male in winter.

Habitat: Rainforest and other wet forests, damp gullies and sometimes gardens.

Breeding: Nest is an untidy cup of shredded bark, rootlets and grass, decorated with moss or lichen; placed in a vertical fork of a tree. Eggs: 2–3.

Distribution: Coastal eastern and south-east mainland, Tasmania and Bass Strait islands. Uncommon resident.

Where to see: Ferntree, Weilangta Forest, Melalueca.

Common Blackbird

Turdus merula

Family: Flycatchers, Thrushes and Whistlers; Muscicapidae

Identification: *250–260mm.* The male is a smart, entirely black bird with an orange-yellow bill and eye-ring. Female has dark brown upperparts with faint pale eyebrow. Underparts are rufous-brown with darker mottlings.

Habits: Occurs singly or in pairs, typically hopping on the ground and vigorously turning over leaves or stabbing the ground aggressively while searching for worms.

Voice: Loud, mellow and serene. Non-repetitive. Sings during breeding season particularly at dawn and dusk. Also a chattering alarm call.

Habitat: Parks, orchards and gardens. Also spreading into forests and scrub.

Breeding: Nest is a bulky cup of dried grass and rootlets, bound with mud lined with fine grass. Built in a dense shrub, in a bank. Eggs: 3–5.

Distribution: Introduced from Europe into the south-east mainland during the 1850s and into Tasmania about 1933. A common resident.

Common Starling

Sturnus vulgaris

Family: Starlings and Mynahs; Sturnidae

Identification: *210–220mm.* A familiar pest of south-east Australia. Male is black overall with an iridescent bronze and purple sheen. Wings and tail have a brown wash. The new autumn plumage is covered in buff speckles. Bill is fine, pointed and dark brown outside the breeding season and turns yellow while breeding. Female is slightly duller.

Habits: Occurs singly or in pairs but usually seen in flocks during winter, sometimes consisting of thousands of birds, which sleep in communal roosts.

Voice: Male sings from a perch while slowly flapping wings. Clicks, wheezes, whistles and thin rattles are interspersed with much mimicry. Also a harsh scolding 'tcheer'.

Habitat: Rural and urban areas, pastoral country, orchards and gardens.

Breeding: Nest is an untidy cup of grass, wool, leaves and feathers in a roof of a building, hole in a cliff or tree hollow. Eggs: 4–5.

Distribution: Unfortunately introduced into south-east mainland during the 1850s and into Tasmania in 1860. Now very numerous and increasing.

Bibliography

Blakers, M., Davies, S.J.J.F. and Reilly, P.N. *The Atlas of Australian Birds,* Melbourne University Press, Victoria. 1984 (currently being revised).

Garnett, S. *National Action Plan for Australian Birds.* Australian National Parks and Wildlife Service, Endangered Species Project No. 121. Canberra, ACT. 1992 (currently being revised).

Green, R.H. *The Fauna of Tasmania: Birds,* Potoroo Publishing, Launceston, Tasmania. 1995.

HANZAB 1990–2000, *Handbook of Australian, New Zealand and Antarctic Birds,* Vols 1–6, Birds Australia, Oxford University Press, Melbourne, Victoria. Vols. 5 and 6 in press.

Lord, G. *A bibliography of ornithology in Tasmania 1950–1993.* Self-published, Sandy Bay, Tasmania. 1994.

Readers Digest Complete Book of Australian Birds, Readers Digest Services, Sydney, NSW.

Ridpath, M.G. and Moreau, R.E. The birds of Tasmania: ecology and evolution, *Ibis* 108: pp. 348–393. 1966.

Sharland, M. *Guide to the Birds of Tasmania,* Drinkwater Publishing, Tasmania. 1981.

Tasmanian Bird Report, *Annual bird report of Birds Tasmania* Vols 1–26, Bird Observer Association of Tasmania. 1971–1997.

Thomas, D. *Tasmanian Bird Atlas. Fauna of Tasmania Handbook No. 2,* University of Tasmania, Hobart, Tasmania. 1979.

Further Information

Birds Australia (National Office)
415 Riversdale Road
Hawthorn East, Victoria 3123

Birds Tasmania (Regional group of Birds Australia)
GPO Box 68
Hobart, Tasmania 7001

Glossary

axillaries feathers covering the 'armpit', i.e. where the underwing joins the body

canopy the uppermost layer of forest vegetation formed by foliage of trees or shrubs

cere fleshy narrow covering of the upper bill containing the nostrils, often coloured

coverts small feathers overlaying the base of larger feathers, e.g. ear, wing (lesser and greater), uppertail (base of rump) and undertail (vent)

covey a small flock, usually of ground birds, e.g. quail

crepuscular active at dusk and/or dawn

culmen ridge along the whole length or top of the beak, i.e. upper beak length

diagnostic distinctive feature (body or behaviour) that clearly identifies the species

display to show or perform ritualised action, e.g. head bobbing, to attract a mate, commence breeding, to strengthen pair bond

dorsal the back surface

eclipse plumage usually dull feathers, aquired by waterfowl and some other birds during winter/non-breeding season

endemic species found naturally in only one country, region or island

estuarine area where fresh water and salt (sea) water intermix

immature sub-adult bird with feathers, after the first moult but before breeding

juvenile birds with their first true feathers grown after their natal down (chick stage)

lamellae stiff comb-like membrane on the inner edge of the bill, used to sieve food particles, e.g. ducks and prions

mandible the upper and lower half of a bird's bill

midden accumulated remains of aboriginal dwelling site or feeding site, often consisting of bone, shell and charcoal fragments

mollymawk general term for smaller species of albatross and giant petrels

pelagic seabirds that spend most of their lives far out to sea and only come ashore to breed

primaries outermost and longest flight feathers on a bird's wing, usually controlling manoeuvrability

Ramsar sites wetland areas recognised as having internationally important values, especially waterfowl and migratory bird sites (ten sites in Tasmania)

scapular shoulder blade or feathers that cover the upper shoulder of the wing

speculum iridescent (often green) patch on the secondary feathers of a duck's wing

sub–terminal near the end or the last before the end, often of the tail

tail band distinctive stripe usually horizontal across the tail feathers

trailing edge hind edge of a flipper or spread wing

understorey vegetation occurring from shrub to ground layer, or beneath tree layer

ventral underside of the body, e.g. belly, as opposed to upper (dorsal) surface

Checklist

Quail, Ducks, Geese & Grebes

Stubble Quail
Coturnix pectoralis
Brown Quail *C. ypsilophora*
California Quail
Callipepla californica
Blue-billed Duck
Oxyura australis
Musk Duck
Biziura lobata
Black Swan
Cygnus atratus
Cape Barren Goose
Cereopsis novaehollandiae
Australasian Shelduck
Tadorna tadornoides
Australian Wood Duck
Chenonetta jubata
Mallard *Anas platyrhynchos*
Pacific Black Duck
A. superciliosa
Australian Shoveler
A. rhynchotis
Grey Teal *A. gracilis*
Chestnut Teal *A. castanea*
Hardhead *Aythya australis*
Australasian Grebe
Tachybaptus novaehollandiae
Hoary-headed Grebe
Poliocephalus poliocephalus
Great Crested Grebe
Podiceps cristatus

Penguins, Petrels, Cormorants & Herons

Little Penguin *Eudyptula minor*
Common Diving-Petrel
Pelecanoides urinatrix
Southern Giant-Petrel
Macronectes giganteus
Northern Giant-Petrel
M. halli
Cape Petrel *Daption capense*
Great-winged Petrel
Pterodroma macroptera
White-headed Petrel
P. lessoni
Antarctic Prion
Pachyptila desolata
Fairy Prion *P. turtur*
Sooty Shearwater
Puffinus griseus
Short-tailed Shearwater
P. tenuirostris
Fluttering Shearwater
P. gavia

Wandering Albatross
Diomedea exulans
Royal Albatross
D. epomophora
Black-browed Albatross
D. melanophris
Shy Albatross *D. cauta*
Yellow-nosed Albatross
D. chlororhynchos
Buller's Albatross
D. bulleri
White-faced Storm-Petrel
Pelagodroma marina
Australasian Gannet
Morus serrator
Little Pied Cormorant
Phalacrocorax melanoleucos
Black-faced Cormorant
P. fuscescens
Little Black Cormorant
P. sulcirostris
Great Cormorant
P. carbo
Australian Pelican
Pelecanus conspicillatus
White-faced Heron
Egretta novaehollandiae
Little Egret *E. garzetta*
Great Egret *Ardea alba*
Cattle Egret *A. ibis*
Nankeen Night Heron
Nycticorax caledonicus
Australasian Bittern
Botaurus poiciloptilus

Birds of Prey

Whistling Kite
Haliastur sphenurus
White-bellied Sea-Eagle
Haliaeetus leucogaster
Swamp Harrier
Circus approximans
Brown Goshawk
Accipiter fasciatus
Grey Goshawk
A. novaehollandiae
Collared Sparrowhawk
A. cirrhocephalus
Wedge-tailed Eagle
Aquila audax
Brown Falcon
Falco berigora
Australian Hobby
F. longipennis
Peregrine Falcon
F. peregrinus
Nankeen Kestrel
F. cenchroides

Rails, Waders,
Gulls & Terns

Lewin's Rail
Rallus pectoralis
Australian Spotted Crake
Porzana fluminea
Spotless Crake
P. tabulensis
Purple Swamphen
Porphyrio porphyrio
Dusky Moorhen
Gallinula tenebrosa
Tasmanian Native-hen
G. mortierii
Eurasian Coot *Fulica atra*
Painted Button-quail
Turnix varia
Latham's Snipe
Gallinago hardwickii
Bar-tailed Godwit
Limosa lapponica
Whimbrel
Numenius phaeopus
Eastern Curlew
N. madagascariensis
Common Greenshank
Tringa nebularia
Grey-tailed Tattler
Heteroscelus brevipes
Ruddy Turnstone
Arenaria interpres
Red-necked Stint
Calidris ruficollis
Curlew Sandpiper
C. ferruginea
Pied Oystercatcher
Haematopus longirostris
Sooty Oystercatcher
H. fuliginosus
Black-winged Stilt
Himantopus himantopus
Pacific Golden Plover
Pluvialis fulva
Red-capped Plover
Charadrius ruficapillus
Double-banded Plover
C. bicinctus
Black-fronted Dotterel
Elseyornis melanops
Hooded Plover
Thinornis rubricollis
Banded Lapwing
Vanellus tricolor
Masked Lapwing *V. miles*
Arctic Jaeger
Stercorarius parasiticus
Pacific Gull *Larus pacificus*
Kelp Gull *L. dominicanus*
Silver Gull
L. novaehollandiae
Caspian Tern
Sterna caspia

Crested Tern *S. bergii*
White-fronted Tern
S. striata
Little Tern *S. albifrons*
Fairy Tern *S. nereis*

Pigeons, Parrots,
Owls & Kingfishers

Spotted Turtle-Dove
Streptopelia chinensis
Common Bronzewing
Phaps chalcoptera
Yellow-tailed Black
Cockatoo
Calyptorhynchus funereus
Brush Bronzewing
P. elegans
Galah *Cacatua roseicapilla*
Long-billed Corella
C. tenuirostris
Little Corella
C. sanguinea
Sulphur-crested Cockatoo
C. galerita
Musk Lorikeet
Glossopsitta concinna
Green Rosella
Platycercus caledonicus
Eastern Rosella
P. eximius
Swift Parrot
Lathamus discolor
Blue-winged Parrot
Neophema chrysostoma
Orange-bellied Parrot
N. chrysogaster
Ground Parrot
Pezoporus wallicus
Pallid Cuckoo
Cuculus pallidus
Fan-tailed Cuckoo
Cacomantis flabelliformis
Horsfield's Bronze Cuckoo
Chrysococcyx basalis
Shining Bronze-Cuckoo
C. plagosus
Southern Boobook
Ninox novaeseelandiae
Masked Owl
Tyto novaehollandiae
Tawny Frogmouth
Podargus strigoides
Australian Owlet-nightjar
Aegotheles cristatus
White-throated Needletail
Hirundapus caudacutus
Azure Kingfisher
Alcedo azurea
Laughing Kookaburra
Dacelo novaeguineae
Superb Lyrebird
Menura novaehollandiae

189

Index

Index